More than 200 delicious new ways to use natural foods and prepare meatless gourmet dishes!

Delicious, attractive, and easy to prepare, a diet of health foods can help you keep slim and feeling younger and more vigorous. These gourmet recipes can also help you to add variety to your meatless menus—and keep the cost of your meals down.

Included, too, is a special section on salt-free cooking to help you to make your salt-free meals tastier than you ever believed possible.

THE GOURMET
HEALTH FOODS
COOKBOOK

(Original title: Mike and Olga's Favorite Recipes)

By Mike and Olga Teichner

Foreword by Erle Stanley Gardner

NEW YORK

We dedicate Book One of this little cookbook to all our friends, also the people who are interested in vegetarian meals.

For her help and patience, we gratefully dedicate Book Two to Mrs. Harpo Marx.

CONTENTS

BOOK ONE, *Magic Without Meat*

BOOK TWO, *Savor Without Salt*

Mike Teichner has a magic with foods.

For a long time this magic has been a carefully guarded trade secret, but now Mike has been prevailed upon by his friends, who have promised overwhelming support, to publish his favorite recipes in the form of a cookbook.

I have known Mike Teichner for several years. He and his wife run a little restaurant in a health food store in Palm Springs.

Health food stores do a good business selling packaged products, vitamins, and health ideas. Quite a few of them have fruit juice bars; but very, very few of them have restaurants where health food dishes are dispensed on the premises.

The real reason for this is that so many of the health food dishes which are so beneficial to the consumer are monotonous to the palate and can't compete for flavor with a good filet mignon.

Mike and his wife, however, are building up quite a business over in Palm Springs, and Palm Springs is a difficult place in which to build up a restaurant business because the city has such a number of fine restaurants that the competition is terrific.

Thirty-five years ago Mike Teichner was a healthy, robust meat cutter. Then suddenly arthritis struck and Mike found himself face to face with a life of crippled inactivity.

Mike is a fighter. He started studying his condition; he found that certain foods agreed with him, that others did not.

In the course of time Mike regained his ability to work. He became what is known as a healthist He ate only the foods which made for health. But since he found those foods were not very appetizing, he started trying to make them more flavorful.

It was a long, slow process. After years of experimentation Mike and Olga, his wife, worked out a series of recipes for vegetarian health dishes which are tempting to the palate and remarkably nourishing.

Personally, I am omnivorous. I eat what tastes good and I have consumed my share of meat dishes.

In Palm Springs I discovered the little restaurant where Mike and Olga serve their luncheons. I noticed that many of the same people were steady customers. I tried the luncheon dishes and was surprised to find how very delicious they were. I began coming back simply because the food tasted so good. Then I found the food was agreeing with me. I still eat meat, but I eat less meat and more and more of Mike's dishes.

From time to time I asked him about how the dishes were made. I had experimented with the canned meat-substitutes but could never find any which could hold a candle to Mike's dishes.

Mike was always courteous but vague.

I found that many of Mike's customers were pressing him for his recipes. Finally, Mike decided to put them all in print. I think he would like to retire one of these days, and the steady repeat business he has built up at his lunch counter has shown him the pulling power of his recipes.

I have eaten all over the world. I love good cooking. More and more frequently I come to Palm Springs to eat at Mike's simply because his dishes are so savory, so satisfying and at the same time so healthful. And for persons who for one reason or another have become vegetarians, Mike's dishes are a godsend.

I feel that once the general public tries Mike and Olga's recipes it will make quite a difference in the eating habits of a large segment of our population.

I hope this book is a great success, but I also hope Mike doesn't retire.

His food tastes too good.

ERLE STANLEY GARDNER

PREFACE

People think it is difficult to prepare vegetarian food. Not with the proper guide. We think this is the key to your problem.

Some recipes are Mike's creation; some are Olga's. But we always talked over our individual ideas to bring out the best of our knowledge to prepare it the most palatable way. We took many courses; studied vegetarian cooking to know the value of the different herbs and vegetables. There is nothing better than garden-fresh vegetables prepared the right and proper way.

If you follow these tested recipes, you will be amazed how easy it will be for you to prepare wholesome meals for your family from just plain vegetables.

We never thought to write up salt-free recipes until Mrs. Harpo Marx gave us the idea. Her late husband, who suffered from a heart condition and required salt-free dishes, said many times, "No dinner is complete for me without your soup." She told us that many people are looking for a salt-free recipe book. We considered this suggestion very seriously.

The recipes in Book Two are very similar to our regular ones. We use salt substitutes in powder form and special herbs and seasonings.

People who patronized our restaurant told us how delicious, tasty, and flavorful the food we served was; and they asked for recipes very often of their favorite dish. We were very much pleased; and to show them our great appreciation, we gathered our best and most favored recipes in one big bouquet and present them with our very best wishes for good health always.

Sincerely,

Mike and Olga Teichner

9

MAGIC WITHOUT MEAT

BOOK ONE

Suggestions

To make a real good dish out of the natural foods or vegetables, you have to use different kinds of herbs and flavorings. They are available in your local health food store.

We may suggest a few which will give you good results:

Savita
Vegex
Savorex
Beef Flavor (imitation)
Yerba Encanta
Sweet Basil
Vegetized Salt
Vegetable Broth Powder
Dill Weed
Rosemary
Sea Salt

All the canned meat substitutes are excellent for roasts and/or any mixed dishes that you desire to make.

For salad dressings, we recommend these two health food mayonnaises:

Lemonaise
Lecinaise

These contain the proper ingredients. Every health food store carries them.

Since we are cooking with very little water, you have to use lids on pots and skillets. When the recipe calls for "simmering," use a low flame.

When you make the thickening of water and flour, mix it to a smooth texture and strain it before you pour in the boiling liquid. Stir constantly to avoid lumpiness.

For baking, the flour should be sifted before measuring.

When you shred apples, always wash and core them first.

When you grind potatoes, put a strainer in the pot. You can shake out the excess liquid this way without much extra effort.

We use very little oil to saute onions, so be sure to stir the onions frequently.

When baking roasts or vegetables, it is best to cover them for the first ½ hour.

Blending is done with an electric blender. Do not use blender with glass top if ingredients are hot.

In shredding vegetables for salads, we recommend the use of a Griscer or Salad Master.

All recipes serve 6 to 8 people unless otherwise specified.

All ovens are pre-heated.

Suggestions

When you make your soup in a blender, for extra delicate taste add one tablespoon cashew nuts — and in the winter time, if you like a heavier soup, put one hard-boiled egg in the mixture.

You can choose other protein ingredients like skim milk powder, soy milk powder, also Brewer's yeast.

It is nice to soak one tablespoon of corn meal in hot water for one hour; add it to the blender along with one tablespoon cashew nuts. It is delicious.

From these suggested items above, choose whatever you like.

It should be liquified *always*.

Avocado pulp — two tablespoons — added in the blender also gives a delicate flavor. Another suggestion — three tablespoons of boiled yams or white potatoes can be put in the blender.

Mushroom Barley Soup

½ cup barley   8 cups of water

Cook the barley in two cups of water until tender. In six cups of water, cook:

½ cup diced carrots   ½ cup diced parsnips
½ cup diced celery   ½ cup chopped onions
½ cup diced celery root

When vegetables are cooked, take out two cups of broth, one cup of vegetables; put in blender and add:

½ tablespoon sea salt   1 tablespoon chopped
½ teaspoon sweet basil   parsley
1 tablespoon cashew nuts   ½ teaspoon Accent
                             1 clove of garlic

Liquify and add to the soup. Also add:

Cooked barley   1 cup chopped
                              fresh mushrooms

Simmer together slowly, stirring constantly since barley sticks easily to the bottom of the pot.

Serve hot with chopped parsley on top.

Brown Onion Soup

4 medium onions, sliced   5 cups water
3 tablespoons Safflower oil   ½ teaspoon sea salt
3 tablespoons whole wheat   ½ teaspoon Accent
   pastry flour   ½ teaspoon Vegex

Brown the onions in 1½ tablespoons of oil. Let cool. Mix the flour in the remaining 1½ tablespoons of oil, heat and add 2 cups of water. Boil slowly. Beat up the onions in the blender with salt, Accent, and the remaining 3 cups of cold water. Combine all ingredients and cook 2 minutes.

Serve hot with whole wheat crackers.

Barley Soup with Leeks

½ cup barley
7 cups water   ½ cup chopped onion
1 cup diced leeks   1 clove garlic, chopped
1 cup diced celery   1 tablespoon salt
1 cup diced parsnips   1 teaspoon Accent
1 cup diced celery roots   2 tablespoons chopped
1 cup diced carrots   parsley

Cook the barley in the 7 cups of water. When it is tender, add remaining ingredients except parsley and cook for 25 minutes longer. Soup will thicken so stir it frequently.

Serve with chopped parsley.

½ cup diced celery root
½ cup diced carrots
½ cup diced parsnips
1 small diced turnip
1 cup diced celery

½ cup finely chopped
 onions
½ cup cut string beans
5 cups water

Simmer all the vegetables in 5 cups of water. *Never* boil. Take out ⅓ of the vegetables and 2 cups broth. Liquify and add:

2 tablespoons cashew nuts
1 teaspoon vegetized salt
1 teaspoon Yerba Encanta
1 clove garlic
1 teaspoon skim milk
 powder

1 teaspoon Accent
1 teaspoon sweet basil
1 tablespoon
 chopped parsley

Liquify until smooth. Add it to the soup.
Serve hot with chopped parsley on top.

Potato Peel Broth, Number 1

1 pound potatoes with nice
 healthy skins
1 medium carrot, unpeeled
2 stalks celery

2 quarts water
½ teaspoon salt
½ teaspoon Yerba
 Encanta

Peel potatoes ½ inch thick and use the peel side only. Cut carrot in half and cut celery into big pieces.

Simmer in water until tender. Then add salt and Yerba Encanta, or for more flavor, a dash of Accent.

Strain, serving only the clear broth.

17

Vegetable Gumbo Soup

1 cup diced celery
1 cup diced carrots
1 cup diced parsnips
½ cup diced celery root
½ cup chopped onions
1 teaspoon sea salt
1 teaspoon Accent

1 teaspoon sweet basil
6 cups water
1 hard-boiled egg
1 clove garlic
¼ cup chopped parsley
½ cup cut okra

Cook all ingredients in water, except okra, garlic, parsley, and egg. Take out ⅓ of the vegetables and 2 cups of the broth. Put it in the blender and add the egg, garlic, and half of the parsley. Blend until smooth and add to the vegetables. Then add the okra and simmer 2 minutes.

Serve hot with the remaining parsley on top.

Potato Peel Broth, Number 2

2 pounds of potatoes
½ green pepper
1 pint cut (large pieces)
celery and celery leaves

1 medium carrot
6 cups water
½ teaspoon Accent
½ teaspoon sea salt

Wash potatoes with vegetable brush. Peel ½ inch thick, don't use center of potatoes.

Put all vegetables in water, cutting is not necessary. Simmer until potatoes are tender. Strain the broth and flavor with Accent and salt.

Navy Bean Soup

9 cups water
1 cup navy beans
½ cup chopped onions
½ cup diced carrots

½ cup diced celery
½ cup diced parsnips
½ cup diced celery root

Soak the beans in three cups of water overnight. Next day add two cups of water and cook until tender with the chopped onions. The other vegetables should be cooked in four cups of water. Take out two cups of the broth, and one cup of the cooked vegetables. Put in the blender and add:

1 teaspoon sea salt	2 tablespoons
1 teaspoon vegetized salt	chopped parsley
½ teaspoon Accent	1 clove garlic
½ teaspoon bacon yeast	2 tablespoons cashew nuts

Liquify until smooth. Add to the cooked beans and vegetables. For more blending variety, see page 13.

Serve hot with chopped parsley on top.

Rice Tomato Soup

5 cups chopped fresh tomatoes	2 cups cold water
½ cup whole wheat pastry flour	½ cup finely chopped onions
	1 tablespoon Safflower oil

Liquify the tomatoes in 1 cup water and boil slowly. Make thickening from the flour and 1 cup cold water, strain and add to the boiled tomato juice.

Saute the onions in the oil, and add:

½ teaspoon Vegex	½ cup finely chopped
½ cup diced green pepper	celery
	½ teaspoon red paprika

Simmer three minutes. Add to the thickened tomato juice. Add:

¼ cup lemon juice	½ cup boiled brown rice
2 rounded tablespoons brown sugar	¼ teaspoon grated lemon rind.
½ tablespoon sea salt	

Serve hot with crackers.

Lima Bean Soup

1 cup lima beans (soaked overnight)	½ cup diced celery
	1 cup diced parsnips
½ cup chopped onions	½ cup diced carrots
8 cups water	

Cook the lima beans separately with the onions in 8 cups of water until almost done. Drop in remaining vegetables and cook slowly for 15 minutes.

Take out 2 cups of broth and 1 cup vegetables, put in the blender. Add:

1 teaspoon vegetized salt	2 tablespoons chopped parsley
½ teaspoon Accent	
½ teaspoon bacon yeast	1 clove garlic
	½ teaspoon sea salt

Liquify until smooth. Add to the beans and vegetables. Serve hot with chopped parsley on top.

Lentil Soup

1 cup dry lentils	1 cup diced parsnips
½ cup chopped onions	½ cup diced celery
8 cups water	½ cup diced carrots

Cook the lentils separately with the onions in 4 cups of water.

Boil the vegetables in four cups of water until tender.

Take out one-third of the vegetables and two cups broth. Put in blender. Add:

½ teaspoon vegetized salt	2 tablespoons chopped parsley
½ teaspoon Accent	
½ teaspoon bacon yeast	1 clove garlic
2 tablespoons cashew nuts	

Liquify until smooth. Combine with the vegetables and the cooked lentils; simmer slowly for two minutes.

Serve hot with chopped parsley.

Split Pea Soup

1½ cups green split peas	½ cup chopped onions
5 cups water	

Soak the peas overnight in two cups of cold water. Next day add 3 cups water and cook until tender with the onions.

½ cup diced carrots	½ cup diced parsnips
½ cup diced celery	4 cups water

Cook carrots, celery, and parsnips in 4 cups of water. When tender, take out half of the vegetables and two cups of broth. Put in blender with:

1 tablespoon sweet basil	1 clove garlic
1 teaspoon Accent	¼ teaspoon bacon yeast
1½ teaspoons sea salt	1 tablespoon parsley

Liquify until smooth. Take:

2 tablespoons Safflower oil	2 tablespoons whole wheat flour

Brown the flour slightly in the oil, add the broth from the rest of the vegetables, stir until smooth; then boil all together with the cooked peas.

Serve hot with whole wheat crackers.

Beet Soup Borscht

6 medium-sized beets
3 tablespoons brown sugar
4 tablespoons lemon juice

½ tablespoon sea salt
4 tablespoons yogurt

Wash and brush the beets well, cover well with water and boil until tender.

Save the broth; slice the beets and put in jar. Season the broth with the sugar, lemon juice, and salt. Pour over the sliced beets. Keep overnight in refrigerator.

Next day put it in the blender, add the yogurt and liquify.

Serve cold with extra yogurt on top.

Fresh Green Pea Soup

1½ cups shelled peas
(save the pods)

2 cups water

Wash the young pods. Liquify in two cups of water and strain. Cook peas for ten minutes. Add:

Strained liquid from the
pods
½ cup diced carrots
½ cup diced parsnips

½ cup diced celery
4 young scallions, chopped
4 cups water

Simmer until tender. Take out two cups of the broth and one cup of the vegetables. Put in blender and add:

1 teaspoon vegetized salt
½ teaspoon Accent
2 tablespoons chopped
parsley

1 clove garlic
2 tablespoons cashew nuts
1 tablespoon brown sugar

Add to balance of vegetables. Simmer together for two minutes.

Serve hot with chopped parsley on top.

Asparagus Soup

1½ pounds asparagus   7 cups water

Cut the tough part of the asparagus, wash well and cook 20 minutes in the 7 cups water. Strain the liquid in a 2 quart saucepan and add:

Asparagus tops, cut in 1   ½ cup diced celery
   inch lengths   ½ cup diced parsnips

Simmer until tender. Take out 2 cups of broth and 1 cup vegetables from the above mixture and blend in the blender. Then add:

½ cup boiled yams   parsley
2 tablespoons cashew nuts   1 teaspoon sea salt
1 small clove garlic   1 teaspoon Accent
1 tablespoon chopped

Liquify in the blender and add to the soup. Simmer 2 minutes.
Serve hot. Makes wonderful light soup.

Cream of Celery Soup

½ cup chopped onions   1 cup diced Russet
3 tablespoons Safflower oil   potatoes
2 cups finely chopped   2 quarts of warm water
   celery   3 tablespoons whole wheat
½ cup diced parsnips   flour
½ cup diced celery root   ½ cup cold water

Saute the onions in the oil, using a 3 quart sauce pan. Add celery, parsnips, celery root, and potatoes. Pour on 2 quarts of water and boil for 25 minutes over low flame. Mix the flour with cold water, strain, add to the boiling soup and simmer for 2 minutes. Remove from fire.

Put 2 cups of soup in the blender, add:

½ cup cashew nuts 1 clove garlic
¼ cup chopped parsley ½ teaspoon sweet basil

Blend smooth, pour into the soup and mix with:

¼ cup chopped parsley ¼ teaspoon Yerba
1 teaspoon sea salt Encanta
1 teaspoon Accent

Serve hot.

Cream of Potato Soup

½ cup sliced onions 2 tablespoons Safflower
oil

Saute the onions and oil in a 2 quart saucepan. Then take:

3 cups diced Russet ½ cup diced parsnips
potatoes ½ cup diced celery root
1 cup diced celery 7 cups warm water

Add the vegetables to the sauteed onion mixture. Heat thoroughly. Then add the warm water and boil about 20 minutes, or until the vegetables are tender.

3 tablespoons Safflower 3 tablespoons whole wheat
oil pastry flour

Heat the oil and flour in a small pan over a low flame for about ½ minute, stirring constantly with a wooden spoon. Then add:

½ teaspoon red paprika 2 tablespoons finely
1 clove garlic, finely chopped parsley
chopped 1½ cups cold water

Mix well. Bring mixture to a boil.

Combine this mixture with the potato soup in the 2 quart saucepan. Simmer together about 1 minute. Then add:

1 teaspoon sea salt	Dash of white pepper
1 teaspoon Accent	

Serve hot.

Potato Salad

4 cups cooked, diced
potatoes (cook potatoes
in jackets, peel and
dice)
½ cup finely chopped
scallions
½ cup diced green pepper
1 cup finely chopped
celery

1 hard-boiled egg,
shredded
4 tablespoons Lecinaise
or mayonnaise
3 tablespoons lemon juice
1 tablespoon water
Sugar and salt to taste
2 tablespoons finely
chopped parsley
1 tablespoon pimiento

Mix all ingredients with one tablespoon parsley. Place
it in a round salad bowl.
Sprinkle the top with the rest of the parsley.
Keep refrigerated until serving time.

Fresh Green Salad

8 leaves of bronze-tipped
lettuce
8 leaves of romaine lettuce
¼ bunch of chicory
lettuce
½ of one butter lettuce

1 cup diced celery
½ diced cucumber
1 tablespoon chopped
fresh peppermint or dill
2 tablespoons chopped
parsley

Wash and chop all the lettuce. Mix all the ingredients
and serve it with your favorite dressing. Top with
chopped parsley.

Tossed Salad

To the above mixture of salad add:

½ cup shredded Jerusalem artichokes	½ cup shredded red cabbage
½ cup shredded carrots	1 cup peeled and diced tomatoes

Toss with French dressing. Top with sunflower seeds.

Sliced Tomato Plate

4 big slices of tomato	2 tablespoons chopped onions
3 romaine lettuce leaves	
4 green pepper rings	1 teaspoon chopped parsley
1 teaspoon Lecinaise	

Arrange the sliced tomatoes on the romaine lettuce leaves. Put on the green pepper rings and the Lecinaise in the center. Sprinkle with chopped onions and parsley. Makes 1 serving.

Mixed Green Salad Plate

Ingredients from Fresh Green Salad recipe	¾ cup beets, shred fine on grater
Cottage cheese or hard-boiled egg & red paprika	Sliced tomatoes
	½ cup crisp alfalfa sprouts
Avocado	Parsley
¾ cup carrots, shred fine on grater	Sunflower seeds

Use the Fresh Green Salad recipe for foundation at bottom of the plate to build up a beautiful salad.

Put a scoop of cottage cheese in the middle of the green salad, surround with four slices of avocado. Arrange two scoops of carrots, two scoops of beets around the plate, put the sliced tomatoes between the carrots and beets.

If you prefer egg, cut it in half, sprinkle with red paprika, in place of the cottage cheese.

Sprinkle with alfalfa sprouts and parsley on top of the carrots and beets.

Serve with French or Roquefort dressing. Top with sunflower seeds.

Egg Salad

3 hard-boiled eggs, shredded
1 teaspoon chopped chives
1 tablespoon finely chopped celery
6 olives, chopped
½ teaspoon Accent
½ teaspoon vegetized salt
2 tablespoons Lecinaise

Mix all ingredients and serve on lettuce leaves garnished with red radishes, carrot sticks, and black olives.

Marinated Green Pepper with Onions

3 cups water
2 tablespoons tarragon
2 tablespoons sweet basil
1 large bay leaf
2 teaspoons salt
4 tablespoons apple cider vinegar
3 tablespoons brown sugar
2½ cups green pepper strips
¾ cup thinly sliced onion
1 clove garlic
1 teaspoon olive oil

Bring water to a boil, add tarragon, sweet basil and bay leaf. Boil 10 minutes and turn off fire. Let soak for 15 minutes, then strain. Add to this liquid the salt, vinegar, and sugar. Make it quite strong. The green pepper and onion go in a jar first. Now add the liquid, garlic, and oil. Put in refrigerator.

The next day shake up the jar and taste the brine. Possibly you need some more flavoring, and in case you need some, take out 1 cup of the brine and add whatever is necessary according to your taste. Let it stay for three days and then it is ready to use.

It is very tasty in potato salad or cole slaw.

Marinated Young Turnips with Onions

Use the herb recipe described in Marinated Green Pepper with Onions for the brine. Take 2 bunches of young turnips, soak ½ hour in water; then wash with a vegetable brush. Boil until soft. Cool and slice thin. Add 1 cup onions, sliced thin.

If you can get a ripe pepper in late fall, it is nice and red. Slice thin and add. It is a very colorful combination and it is delicious.

Nice to serve with everything.

Cole Slaw

1 pound green cabbage	1 teaspoon salt
½ cup grated carrots	2 tablespoons brown sugar
½ cup diced green pepper	½ cup chopped parsley
½ cup lemon juice	2 tablespoons Safflower
2 tablespoons water	oil

Shred the cabbage finely. Mix in all ingredients. Keep refrigerated until serving time.

If you desire Lemonaise or mayonnaise, mix in two tablespoons, top with chopped parsley.

For variety, you can mix in crushed pineapple, leaving out the carrot and green pepper, mayonnaise and parsley. Or use grated apples, leaving out the carrot, green pepper and parsley as well as the mayonnaise.

Mixed Salad

½ cup lemon juice
2 tablespoons Safflower oil
2 tablespoons brown sugar
½ teaspoon vegetized salt
2 tablespoons water
1 cup finely sliced, unpeeled cucumbers
½ cup shredded cauliflower

1 cup finely chopped green peppers
1 cup finely chopped celery
½ cup finely chopped scallions
½ clove garlic, chopped finely or pressed
6 leaves of romaine lettuce, chopped

Make a dressing of the lemon juice, oil, sugar, salt, and water. Toss the salad and garnish with:

1 shredded carrot
1 sliced avocado

Fresh dill weed

Mixed Vegetable Salad

Here is a wonderful salad — it is a meal by itself — a nice, fresh bronze and butter lettuce salad bowl, and, if you like, watercress. Now, you can choose from aromatic herbs — mint, spearmint, dill weed, marjoram. Chop up everything and mix. If you like a little aroma of garlic, rub the bottom of the mixing bowl with a garlic bud.

If you want to make individual plates, spread the salad on the plates, sprinkle on a little crushed pineapple. If you have a salad master or any other of this type of shredder, use the finest shredder for carrots, beets and young turnips.

The center of the plate is for a scoop of cottage cheese, egg salad or Nuttose, with a little yogurt topping.

31

Around the edges of the plates, put small piles of shredded vegetables. Alternate the colors. Alfalfa sprouts are very nice around the edges. (I will tell you later how to raise it.) Place small tomato wedges between the shredded vegetables. Cut avocado slices, and place around the cheese. Sprinkle sunflower seeds or raw cashew nuts on the salad along with some chopped parsley. Now you have a colorful salad.

Nuttose Salad

1 small can Nuttose meat substitute, diced finely	¼ cup chopped scallions
	½ cup mayonnaise
1 cup chopped celery	1 teaspoon Accent
1 cup chopped green pepper	½ teaspoon vegetized salt

Mix all ingredients and serve on lettuce bed, garnished with wedged tomatoes, black olives, and topped with chopped parsley.

Fruit Salad

1 grapefruit	2 dates
2 oranges	1 apple (sliced)
½ papaya	1 banana (sliced)
Lettuce leaves	Honey
1 pear (sliced)	1 tablespoon cashew nuts
4 steamed prunes	or pecans

Peel and slice grapefruit, oranges and papaya.
Arrange on plate on lettuce leaves.
Arrange the rest of the fruit and top with honey and chopped nuts.

Green Cabbage and Apple Salad

¼ cup lemon juice
1 cup shredded apples
2 cups of shredded cabbage
½ cup diced celery
½ cup finely chopped walnuts

1 tablespoon Safflower oil
2 tablespoons sugar
Pinch of salt
1 tablespoon chopped parsley

Pour some lemon juice on the shredded apple to prevent discoloration. Mix all ingredients except parsley.

Arrange the salad in a bowl and top with the freshly cut parsley.

Red Cabbage Slaw

Cut about 3 cups of cabbage on a salad master, or, if you are a good cutter, use a knife. Salt it down with 1 tablespoon salt. Add 2 tablespoons of chopped chives or green scallions — finely chopped. If you like apple cider or half vinegar and half lemon juice, it gives a very nice aroma. Add sugar to taste and olive oil (about 3 tablespoons) and mix well.

Cool for half an hour, and now it is ready to serve.

Cucumber Salad

1 large cucumber, sliced thin on shredder
½ cup thin sliced onions
½ cup sliced green pepper
1 clove garlic, pressed or chopped
¼ teaspoon sea salt

1 tablespoon chopped dill weed
1 tablespoon chopped parsley
3 tablespoons lemon juice
1 tablespoon brown sugar
2 tablespoons cold water
3 tablespoons yogurt

Mix all ingredients. Keep refrigerated until serving time.

6 leaves of romaine lettuce	4 dates, cut into small
½ cup chopped celery	pieces
¼ cup shredded carrot	1 tablespoon raisins
1 cup shredded apple	1 tablespoon chopped
	pecans

Wash and chop the romaine lettuce. Arrange on bottom of the plate and follow with one layer each of the ingredients. Top with the raisins and pecans.

Serve with yogurt dressing (see Dressings). Makes 2 servings.

French Dressing, Number 1

1 pint mayonnaise
1 pint tomato juice
1 tablespoon soy sauce
3 tablespoons apple cider
   vinegar
½ teaspoon vegetized salt

1 tablespoon tarragon
1 tablespoon sweet basil
1 small piece garlic
2 tablespoons brown sugar
1 tablespoon fresh dill
   weed

Put all ingredients in blender and work it to a smooth texture.
Serve cold on salads.

French Dressing, Number 2

¾ cup mayonnaise
1 cup tomato juice
¼ cup lemon juice
1 clove garlic

2 tablespoons sugar
¼ teaspoon salt
2 tablespoons chopped
   fresh dill weed

Put all ingredients in the blender and work until smooth.
Serve cold on salads.

Roquefort Dressing

1 cup yogurt
½ cup buttermilk
2 tablespoons lemon juice
1 teaspoon brown sugar

¼ teaspoon sea salt
½ clove garlic, pressed
6 tablespoons shredded
   Roquefort cheese

Put the yogurt in a mixing bowl and beat smooth with wire eggbeater. Combine all ingredients and mix well.
Serve cold on salads.

Yogurt Dressing

1 cup yogurt   2 tablespoons honey
½ cup coconut milk   1 tablespoon lemon juice

Mix the ingredients to a smooth texture.
Serve cold on fruit or vegetable salads.

Potato Pancakes

½ cup chopped onions
1 tablespoon Safflower oil
2 cups finely grated, peeled
  raw potatoes (Russet or
  Idaho)
½ cup and 1 tablespoon
  whole wheat flour

¼ cup finely chopped
  parsley
2 eggs, well beaten
½ teaspoon Accent
½ teaspoon sea salt
¼ teaspoon white pepper
½ teaspoon baking
  powder

Saute the onions in oil and cool. Add to the peeled, grated potatoes. Mix in remaining ingredients. Drop by spoonfuls on a well-oiled hot skillet. Brown on both sides.

Serve with yogurt or apple sauce. Yield: fourteen little cakes.

Potato Pancakes Deluxe

2 cups finely ground
  potatoes with peelings
½ cup skim milk
½ cup cashew nuts
2 tablespoons finely
  chopped chives or
  scallions
2 eggs, well beaten
1 tablespoon finely
  chopped parsley

1 tablespoon cornmeal
1 tablespoon shredded
  carrot
½ teaspoon M.S.G. or
  Accent
½ teaspoon sea salt
Dash of white pepper
½ cup Rusket crumbs

Use Idaho or Burbank potatoes, wash them well with a vegetable brush and grind, keeping a bowl under the grinder. Shake the liquid out as well as possible.

37

Put milk in liquifier and whip with the cashew nuts.

Put potatoes in mixing bowl, add all ingredients except the crumbs. Mix. Then add the crumbs and blend. Cover and let stand 15 minutes.

Heat a well-oiled heavy skillet and drop by table-spoonsful, making small pancakes. Lightly brown on both sides. Continue until all batter is used.

Makes about 16 pancakes.

Serve with the suggested toppings:

Fresh apple sauce: Core, wash and shred 4 apples. Put in blender with ¼ cup 100% pure maple syrup, ¼ cup lemon juice, pinch of salt, and blend until smooth.

Honeyed peanut butter: Mix well ½ cup honey, ½ cup warm water and ¼ cup peanut butter. This is a tasty topping.

Yogurt Honey topping: 1 cup yogurt, ⅓ cup honey, mix well.

For those who wish an unsweet topping: Put a cup of yogurt in a bowl, mix well with scoop of cottage cheese, sprinkle with red paprika (for more zest add dash of cayenne pepper), add vegetized salt according to your taste.

Cheese Blintzes

2 eggs	1 cup and 2 tablespoons
1 cup whole wheat pastry	water
flour	1 tablespoon Safflower oil
	Dash of salt

Beat the eggs a few seconds in the blender. Add remaining ingredients. Make a smooth batter. Use a six-inch skillet, wipe with Safflower oil by using paper towel. Pour only enough batter, using a 2 ounce ladle, to make a thin pancake, tipping pan side to side to cover the bottom. Bake on both sides to golden brown. When all the batter is made into pancakes, fill the center of each pancake with the following mixture:

1 pound cottage cheese pressed through a strainer
2 egg yolks
¾ cup Rusket crumbs

Few drops of almond extract
1 teaspoon vanilla extract
Sugar and salt to taste

Roll the pancakes. Arrange on serving dish and top with yogurt and cinnamon mixed with brown sugar.

Vegeburger

½ cup finely chopped onions
1 small clove garlic
½ cup finely chopped mushrooms
2 tablespoons Safflower oil
1 can or 1 pound meat

substitute (dark type)
2 slices bread (soaked in water, squeezed)
2 eggs, well beaten
½ cup Rusket crumbs
½ teaspoon Accent
½ teaspoon sweet basil

Saute onions, garlic, and mushrooms in oil. Grind together with meat substitute and bread. Beat up eggs, pour into mixture, adding crumbs, Accent, and sweet basil. Mix well and let stand for 15 minutes.

Make patties of the burger mixture and grill (both sides) in a well-oiled heavy skillet.

Suggested uses for burger patties:

Toast bun, spread with Lecinaise, slice of onion, pattie, lettuce or alfalfa sprouts, sliced tomatoes, and vegetized salt.

If you want a Cheeseburger, when you turn burger in skillet, put a slice of Cheddar cheese on and cover. When the cheese is melted, serve as Burger above.

Serve with Baked Soya Beans (see Entrees).

Serve on bed of rice, prepared as follows:

2 tablespoons sweet butter
1½ cups rice

4½ cups warm water
½ teaspoon sea salt

Melt butter in 2 quart sauce pan. Add rice; heat thoroughly over low flame, stirring constantly. Add warm water and salt. Cover and cook slowly for 1 hour. Set aside for 15 minutes. Then add:

1 tablespoon finely chopped chives	1 teaspoon rosemary
	½ teaspoon Accent

Stuffed Green Pepper

1 Number 2 can meat substitute	¾ cup cooked brown rice
½ cup chopped onions	½ cup peeled and diced tomatoes
½ teaspoon Vegex	Salt to taste
2 tablespoons Safflower oil	Sugar to taste
½ cup chopped celery	½ clove garlic, chopped
6 medium-sized green peppers	2 cups tomato juice
½ cup chopped fresh mushrooms	1½ cups cold water
	3 tablespoons whole wheat flour

Grind the meat substitute. Saute half of the onions and Vegex in half of the oil. Add half of the celery. Cut the top off the green peppers and core out the seeds. Wash and drain the water out. Chop the tops of the green peppers, and add half to the onion mixture, together with the mushrooms and rice. Mix in the ground meat substitute, and fill the green peppers.

Saute the other half of the onions in a casserole. Add the vegetables and the peeled tomatoes, a pinch of salt, garlic, and 1 cup of water. When this is boiling, arrange the stuffed peppers in the casserole, cover and boil slowly for 20 minutes.

Pour over the 2 cups of tomato juice and when it starts to boil, make a thickening of the ½ cup of water and flour. Simmer a few minutes until you have the desired thickness. Salt and sugar to taste.

Pizza Dough

½ cup corn meal
2 tablespoons dry yeast
2 cups warm water
1 cup whole wheat flour

½ cup skim milk powder
¼ cup rice polish
¼ cup soya flour
¼ teaspoon salt

Soften the corn meal in ½ cup of warm water, also soften the dry yeast in ½ cup of warm water. In a mixing bowl, sift together whole wheat flour, skim milk powder, rice polish, and soya flour, add salt and 1 cup of warm water. Add the softened corn meal and yeast.

Make a rather hard dough, knead a few minutes and cover with a towel and let it rise about an hour.

Take two ten-inch pizza trays and sprinkle them with corn meal. Roll out half of the dough at a time and make two pies. You can freeze one if you are not using both.

Bake until crisp for 35 minutes in 350 degree oven. Prick dough with a fork before baking.

Sauce for the Pizza

2 cups tomato puree
1 cup tomato juice
3 tablespoons whole wheat
  flour

½ cup cold water
2 cups grated Cheddar
  cheese

Boil the tomato puree and juice. Make thickening from flour and water. Then add:

1 cup chopped
  mushrooms
½ cup chopped green
  pepper
½ cup chopped olives
½ cup lemon juice
2 tablespoons sugar
1 teaspoon sea salt

¼ teaspoon Yerba
  Encanta
1 teaspoon sweet basil
½ teaspoon red paprika
Pinch of cayenne pepper
1 clove of garlic,
  chopped
3 tablespoons catsup
1 teaspoon Accent

41

Let it boil.

Simmer for 5 minutes, then pour over the baked pizza.

Sprinkle with grated cheese and return to oven and bake until the sauce gets hot and the cheese melts.

Serve hot.

Chili and Beans

½ cup chopped onions
1 tablespoon Safflower oil
½ cup chopped celery
½ cup chopped green pepper
½ cup chopped fresh mushrooms
1 clove garlic, pressed
½ teaspoon vegetized salt
¼ teaspoon Vegex
1 teaspoon 100% maple syrup
Dash cayenne pepper
1 small can vegetarian chili and beans
1 small can garbanzo or kidney beans
Chives or 1 small onion

Saute onions in 1 tablespoon Safflower oil. Add remaining ingredients and heat together with chili and beans.

Serve hot, topped with chives or chopped onions.

Makes 4 servings.

Swiss Steak

2 eggs
1 can Steaklets
1 cup whole wheat bread crumbs
2 tablespoons cornmeal
½ teaspoon sea salt
½ teaspoon Accent
½ teaspoon sweet basil
Paprika

Beat the eggs in a bowl. Drain the Steaklets, dip one by one in the egg batter, then in the bread crumbs combined with the cornmeal, salt, Accent, sweet basil and

42

dash of paprika. Lightly brown both sides in a well-oiled skillet. Arrange the Steaklets in a baking dish.

½ cup chopped onions
1 tablespoon Safflower oil
¼ teaspoon Vegex
1 clove garlic, chopped
½ cup diced green
  pepper

½ cup chopped celery
1 cup peeled and diced
  tomatoes
½ cup chopped fresh
  mushrooms
1 cup water

Saute the onions in the oil, add Vegex, garlic, and all the chopped vegetables and a little salt. Pour on 1 cup water, boil slowly three minutes, then pour over Steaklets. Bake in moderate oven one-half hour at 275 degrees. Special Sauce for Swiss Steak (see Tomato Sauce).

Walnut Loaf

¼ cup chopped onions
2 tablespoons Safflower oil
½ cup chopped celery
¾ cup chopped fresh
  mushrooms

½ cup chopped green
  pepper
½ cup water
3 eggs

Saute the onions in the oil, add celery, mushrooms, and green pepper. Cover and steam for a few minutes in ½ cup water. Beat the eggs in a mixing bowl and add:

1 cup walnuts, cut into
  big pieces
1 cup ground walnuts
1 cup Rusket crumbs
1 cup skim milk
¼ cup skim milk powder

¾ teaspoon salt
1 small can or 2 cups
  Nuteena, ground
2 tablespoons Safflower oil
1 teaspoon Accent

Mix with onions and other ingredients and bake in an eight-by-nine inch oiled baking dish 1½ hours in 300 degree oven until set.
Serve with Country Gravy (see Sauces).

Chile and Kidney Beans

¾ cup chopped onions
2 tablespoons Safflower oil
½ teaspoon red paprika
½ cup chopped green
  pepper
1 cup peeled and diced
  tomatoes
12 black olives, pitted and
  sliced
½ cup chopped
  mushrooms

1 clove garlic, pressed
1 tablespoon brown sugar
1 bay leaf
½ teaspoon Accent
1 small can vegetarian
  chili
1 small can red kidney
  beans
Dash of rosemary

Saute the onions in the oil. Add all ingredients in order. Mix well. Pour into an oiled eight or nine inch baking dish. Cover and bake in moderate oven, 325 degrees, for 35 minutes.

Baked Soya Bean and Rice Loaf

½ cup onions
2 tablespoons soy bean
  oil
½ teaspoon Savita
1 Number 2 can soya beans
  with tomato sauce
2 cups cooked brown
  rice
2 hard-boiled eggs,
  shredded

1 cup coarsely chopped
  pecans
½ teaspoon salt
2 tablespoons Safflower
  margarine
½ cup chopped green
  pepper
½ cup tomato juice
½ teaspoon sweet basil
1 tablespoon brown sugar
1 clove garlic, chopped

Saute the onions in the oil, add remaining ingredients, blend well.

Bake in eight-by-fourteen inch greased baking dish in moderate oven, 300 degrees, until the juices are absorbed.

Serve with Tomato Sauce (see Sauces).

44

⅓ cup chopped onion
½ teaspoon Savita
1 cup chopped celery
⅓ cup chopped green
  pepper
¾ cup shredded and
  peeled sweet potato

3 tablespoons oil
1 teaspoon sea salt
1 teaspoon Accent
1 can or 2 cups good
  quality burger

Saute the onion, Savita, celery, green pepper, sweet potato in the oil. Add salt, Accent. Grind the burger only. Put all in mixing bowl and add:

1½ cups rolled oats
1 cup blanched almonds,
  ground
12 ounces milk
Few drops almond extract

1½ teaspoons sweet basil
3 eggs
1½ teaspoons Yerba
  Encanta

Mix well. Put in well-oiled loaf pan.
Bake 1 hour at 300 degrees.

Egg and Brown Rice Casserole

1¼ cups brown rice
3 cups water
5 hard-boiled eggs, diced
3 tablespoons chopped
  chives
½ cup chopped pecans
1 cup chopped celery
½ cup chopped black
  olives
½ cup grated sharp
  Cheddar cheese

½ cup yogurt
1 cup milk
3 tablespoons Safflower oil
1 teaspoon sea salt
1 teaspoon Accent
1½ cups Rusket crumbs
½ stick Safflower
  margarine
1½ teaspoon tarragon
  leaves

Cover and cook rice in 3 cups of water until tender. Put into a mixing bowl. Add all ingredients except Rusket crumbs and oil. Cut in margarine in small pieces.

Add tarragon leaves pulverized between your palms. Mix gently and put in a lightly oiled casserole dish. Top with the Rusket crumbs which have been moistened with the Safflower oil. Bake in moderate oven, 300 degrees, until set and the crumbs are a golden brown.

Lentil Loaf

1 cup dry lentils
2½ cups water
¾ cup chopped onions
2 tablespoons Safflower oil
½ teaspoon Savita
½ cup chopped green
  pepper
¾ cup chopped walnuts

1 cup tomato juice
½ teaspoon sweet basil
1¼ cups Rusket crumbs
1 clove garlic, chopped
1 teaspoon Accent
½ teaspoon salt
2 eggs, well beaten

Cook the lentils in the 2½ cups water until all the liquid is absorbed. Saute the onions in the oil, add Savita and mix well.

In a mixing bowl, blend together lentils and all the ingredients in order.

Bake in oiled loaf pan at 300 degrees for 45 minutes until set.

Potato Casserole

1½ pounds White Rose
  potatoes
2 tablespoons margarine
2 tablespoons whole wheat
  flour
1 pint milk

½ teaspoon salt
4 ounces Cheddar cheese,
  grated
2 tablespoons chopped
  chives
½ teaspoon red paprika

46

Boil the potatoes in their jackets, cool, peel, and slice.

Melt the margarine in a sauce pan. Mix in flour and heat well. Add milk, mix, boil and stir to a smooth texture. Add salt and grated cheese and let it melt.

Arrange the sliced potatoes in a baking pan, sprinkle with the chives, pour on cheese sauce, and sprinkle with red paprika. Bake in moderate oven, 300 degrees, until top is golden brown.

Millet Loaf

1 ½ cups millet
4 cups water
1 cup chopped onions
3 tablespoons Safflower oil
½ teaspoon Vegex
2 cups finely diced celery
1 cup shredded jikima
½ cup shredded carrots
2 cups milk
1 cup ground cashew nuts
1 cup chopped green pepper

⅓ cup chopped parsley
1 tablespoon wheat germ
1 tablespoon Torumel yeast powder
1 clove garlic, chopped fine
1 tablespoon poultry seasoning
½ teaspoon sea salt
1 teaspoon Accent
2 eggs, well beaten

Cook the millet in 3 cups of water until tender and have absorbed all the water. Set aside and cover.

Saute onions in the oil, add Vegex, celery, jikima and carrot. Pour on 1 cup water, cover and simmer until transparent (don't over cook).

Put millet in a mixing bowl, add steamed onion mixture, milk, cashew nuts, all the seasonings. Mix well and bake in eight-by-fourteen inch well-oiled baking dish for 1 hour, until top is golden brown.

Serve with Mushroom Sauce (see Sauces).

1 cabbage
1 can sauerkraut
½ cup finely chopped
  onions
1 tablespoon Safflower oil
½ cup brown rice
2 cups water
1 can or 1 cup
  Vegeburger
1 egg

1 small clove garlic
½ teaspoon sweet basil
½ teaspoon Accent
½ teaspoon bacon yeast
½ cup finely chopped
  celery
½ cup finely chopped
  green pepper
1 teaspoon salt

Core the cabbage first, then put it in boiling water. When the outer leaves get tender, take out 8 cabbage leaves one by one. The rest of the cabbage chop up and mix with the sauerkraut.

Saute the onions in Safflower oil. Cook the rice separately in one cup water on low flame 40 minutes. Mix all the ingredients in a bowl, except the sauerkraut. Roll a portion of the mixture in each cabbage leaf. Make a layer of the sauerkraut in the bottom of a roaster and a layer of the stuffed cabbage leaves, then cover with the rest of the sauerkraut. Pour on the following mixture:

2 cups water
1 cup tomato juice
1 tablespoon finely
  chopped onions

2 tablespoons brown sugar
2 tablespoons honey
½ teaspoon salt
2 bay leaves

Cover and bake 1½ hours in the oven at 275 degrees.

Serve with Tomato Sauce (see Sauces).

Mock Lamb Roast

1 cup chopped onions
4 tablespoons Safflower oil
½ teaspoon Savita
2 cups finely diced
  celery
1 cup shredded carrot
½ cup small diced green
  pepper
½ cup shredded celery
  root
1 clove garlic, pressed or
  finely chopped
1½ cups warm water
1 pound string green beans

1 cup blanched ground
  almonds
3 eggs, well beaten
½ cup skim milk
1 cup rolled oats
1 tablespoon wheat germ
1 teaspoon sea salt
1 teaspoon Accent
½ teaspoon sweet basil
½ teaspoon poultry
  seasoning
¼ cup chopped parsley
1 cup Rusket flakes

Saute the onions in half of the oil, mix in Savita. Add celery, carrot, green pepper, celery root, and garlic. Pour on ½ cup water, cover and simmer 10 minutes. The vegetables stay crisp.

Wash and parboil the beans in remaining 1 cup water until all liquid is absorbed. Grind beans coarse or chop fine.

In a mixing bowl, add all ingredients in order, except Rusket flakes. Mix well. Fold in eight-by-fourteen inch baking dish, oiled with remaining oil. Top with Rusket flakes. Cover and bake in 300 degree oven for 30 minutes. Remove cover and bake another 30 minutes until well set.

Vegeburger Hash

½ cup chopped onions
2 tablespoons Safflower oil
1 cup vegetable broth (see
  Potassium Broth recipe)
2 cups grated raw potatoes
½ cup chopped green
  peppers

1 clove garlic, pressed
½ teaspoon Accent
½ teaspoon sweet basil
½ teaspoon salt
1 small can or 2 cups
  Vegeburger, grated or
  mashed

49

Saute the onions in the oil. Add all ingredients and mix well. Pour into a well-oiled eight-by-nine inch baking dish, cover and bake in 350 degree oven for 20 minutes, then lower heat to 300 degrees and bake 30 minutes longer.

Use a wide spatula or turner to lift up from pan.

Baked Carrots and Yams

1½ pounds carrots
1 pound yams
4 medium eggs
1 cup milk

3 tablespoons melted
margarine
⅓ stick Safflower
margarine

Peel and parboil the carrots. Cook the yams in their jackets — not too well done. Then peel them. Grate the carrots and the yams. Beat the eggs and milk in a mixing bowl. Then add:

4 tablespoons brown sugar
1 teaspoon sea salt

¼ teaspoon ground
cinnamon

Also add the shredded carrots and yams and mix well.

Pour into an eight-by-nine inch baking dish lined with margarine. Dot with ⅓ stick Safflower margarine and bake 30 minutes in a moderate oven, 300 degrees, until set.

Mock Lamb Patties

1 cup chopped onions
1 tablespoon Safflower oil
3 cups cut string beans
1 cup diced celery
1½ cups water

1 clove of garlic
½ teaspoon Accent
½ cup blanched
almonds

Saute the onions in the oil. Add string beans and celery and 1½ cups water. Cook for 15 minutes. Strain and save the juice. When cooled, grind with the garlic, Accent, and almonds. Then add:

1 egg, well beaten	¼ cup chopped parsley
1 cup cracker crumbs	½ teaspoon sweet basil
½ teaspoon sea salt	

Mix well and form 12 patties. Then beat:

1 egg	¼ cup milk

Combine:

1 cup cracker crumbs	Pinch of red paprika
½ teaspoon Accent	¼ teaspoon rosemary

Dip patties one by one into each mixture — first into the egg mixture, then into the cracker crumb mixture.

Arrange the patties in a well-oiled baking dish. Then pour on the vegetable juice.

Bake in a moderate oven, 350 degrees, for 35 minutes until top is a light brown.

Serve with Mushroom Sauce (see Sauces).

Kasha Balls

1½ cups buckwheat, whole groats	1 teaspoon sea salt
1 cup millet	1 teaspoon Accent
5 cups water	1 clove garlic, pressed or finely chopped
1 cup finely chopped onions	½ teaspoon Vegex
1½ cups finely chopped celery	1 tablespoon mixed herbs
1 cup finely diced green peppers	2 tablespoons skim milk powder
½ cup chopped fresh mushrooms	2 eggs
	½ cup bread crumbs

Cook the buckwheat and millet in separate pans with 2 cups of water on each until tender. Saute the onions in a well-oiled skillet; add all the seasonings, skim milk, and chopped celery and mushrooms and green pepper. Add 1 cup water and simmer 10 minutes. Pulverize the herbs between your palms for better flavor. Put the cooked buckwheat and millet in a mixing bowl. Beat in 2 eggs, and the sauteed onions. Sprinkle with ½ cup crumbs and mix well.

2 eggs	Accent
2 cups bread crumbs	2 tablespoons Safflower oil
½ cup corn meal	Parsley
Salt	

Beat the eggs in a separate bowl. Combine bread crumbs and corn meal. Add a little salt and Accent.

Form little balls from the mixture and dip into egg batter, then roll in the bread crumbs. Fry in hot oil on both sides until golden brown.

Serve with Country Gravy (see Sauces), topped with chopped parsley.

Vegetable Stew

1 cup sliced onions	1 cup largely diced potatoes
2 tablespoons Safflower oil	1 cup diced yams
1 cup largely diced carrots	1 cup sliced fresh mushrooms
1 cup largely diced zucchini	15 chopped olives
1 cup largely diced turnips	1 small can or 1 cup meat substitute
1 cup largely cut celery	2 tablespoons whole wheat flour
2 cups water	½ cup cold water
1 bay leaf	Parsley
Accent	
1 tablespoon salt	

Cook zucchini separately in ½ cup water. Saute the onions in the oil, add carrots, turnips and celery with two cups of water. Cook until tender with the bay leaf and a little salt and Accent added.

Cook the potatoes separately in their jackets; peel, dice and add to the cooked vegetables — also the mushrooms and olives. Simmer two minutes. Then add meat substitute and yam, cooked in jacket, peeled and diced.

Using whole wheat flour and cold water, make a thickening. Add to the simmering vegetables. Let simmer two more minutes.

Serve hot with Country Gravy (see Sauces) and chopped parsley.

Chop Suey

1 cup brown rice	3 cups hot water
2 tablespoons Safflower oil	

Toast the rice in the oil. Add the water, cover and cook very slowly until tender.

2 cups carrot strips	2 cups hot water

Cook 10 minutes, then add:

1 teaspoon Accent	1 cup jikima, cut into
1 teaspoon salt	thin strips
2 cups celery, cut crosswise in strips	

Cook until tender, then add:

1 cup sliced onions	2 tablespoons soy sauce

Simmer 3 more minutes.

Arrange the cooked rice in a deep serving dish, cover with the cooked vegetables, then add:

1 small can Worthington
chicken meat substitute
(cut into thin strips)

Serve with Mushroom Sauce (see Sauces) and top with:

1 cup raw bean sprouts   Fresh pimiento
½ cup diced green pepper

Soya Bean Dishes

Soya beans are very good protein food, low in starch, and add a wonderful item to your daily meal. You can enjoy them often.

Baked Soya Beans with Tomato Sauce

½ cup onions
2 tablespoons Safflower oil
½ cup chopped celery
½ cup chopped green
  pepper
1 bay leaf

½ teaspoon salt
1 cup tomato sauce
1 tablespoon sugar
Dash of red paprika
1 Number 2 can soya
  beans

Saute the onions in the oil. Add all ingredients except soya beans. Simmer 5 minutes, add soya beans. Mix and pour it into eight-by-nine inch baking dish.

Bake in moderate oven, 300 degrees, for about 45 minutes until the liquid is absorbed.

Baked Rice, Number 1

1 cup brown rice
3 cups water
½ cup chopped onions
1 tablespoon Safflower oil
½ cup diced celery
½ cup chopped parsley
½ cup chopped green
  pepper
¼ cup chopped green
  olives

¼ cup chopped fresh
  mushrooms
1 cup tomato juice
1 clove garlic, pressed or
  chopped
2 eggs
1 teaspoon oregano
½ teaspoon sea salt
½ teaspoon Accent

Simmer rice in 3 cups water until tender. Saute onions in Safflower oil, add remaining ingredients to the cooked rice.

Blend well and pour into an eight-by-nine inch oiled baking dish.

Cover and bake in moderate oven about ¾ hour at 275 degrees.

Baked Vegetable Stew

½ cup diced carrots
1 cup diced yams
½ cup diced White Rose potatoes
½ cup diced jikima
1 small diced turnip
½ cup diced celery
1 small onion, cut
4 cups vegetable broth (see Potassium Broth recipe)

½ cup cold water
2 tablespoons whole wheat pastry flour
1 teaspoon sea salt
½ teaspoon Accent
2 tablespoons chopped parsley
2 tablespoons chopped chives

Peel carrots, yam, potatoes, and jikima before dicing. Wash and dice turnip.

Arrange vegetables in an eight-by-nine inch baking dish. Pour on 2 cups of vegetable broth. Cover and bake in a 300 degree oven for 45 minutes.

Make a sauce from the remaining 2 cups of broth. Make thickening with the cold water and flour, strain and pour into the boiling broth, stirring constantly — to the right texture (not too thick). Season with salt and Accent. Pour over baked vegetables. Sprinkle with parsley and chives. Put back into oven for 10 minutes.

Salisbury Steak

¾ cup chopped onions
½ cup chopped green
  pepper
½ cup chopped
  mushrooms

½ cup chopped celery
1 clove garlic, finely
  chopped
1 small can or 2 cups
  Proteena

Saute onions, green peppers, mushrooms, celery, garlic.
Grind Proteena and mix. Then add:

½ cup ground walnuts
2 tablespoons oil
2 eggs, well beaten
1 teaspoon salt

½ teaspoon sage
½ teaspoon Accent
½ teaspoon thyme
½ cup bread crumbs

Make oval-shaped patties, and add 1 cup of water in
the baking dish.
Cover and bake 45 minutes at 300 degrees.
Serve with Tomato Sauce topping (see Sauces).

Vegetable Roast

½ cup chopped onions
1 tablespoon Safflower oil
1 small can or 1 cup
  Vegeburger (ground)
½ cup diced green
  pepper
1 cup shredded raw yams
½ cup ground pecans
¾ cup Rusket crumbs
½ teaspoon sea salt

2 eggs, well beaten
1 clove garlic, pressed or
  chopped finely
1 teaspoon sweet basil
1 teaspoon Accent
½ cup cooked green peas
½ cup cooked diced
  carrots
½ cup cooked diced
  celery

Saute the onions in one tablespoon of Safflower oil,
add all remaining ingredients. Mix well.
Bake in loaf pan one hour at 300 degrees until set.
Serve with your favorite sauce.

Mock Turkey

¾ cup chopped onions
4 tablespoons margarine
1½ cups chopped celery
1½ cups bread crumbs
1 small can or 1 cup
   light-colored meat
   substitute

1 cup ground pecans
2 hard-boiled eggs,
   ground
1 cup skim milk

Saute the onions in the margarine. Add celery and bread crumbs, toasted together 3 minutes. Add ground meat substitute, pecans, milk, and hard-boiled eggs. Then add:

1 teaspoon poultry
   seasoning
½ teaspoon sage
1 teaspoon Accent

1 teaspoon sea salt
1 tablespoon Yerba
   Encanta

Mix well. Bake in well-oiled eight-by-nine inch baking dish at 300 degrees for 45 minutes.

Serve with Country Gravy (see Sauces).

Enchiladas

3 eggs
⅔ cup water
⅓ cup tomato juice
2 tablespoons Safflower oil
¼ teaspoon salt

½ teaspoon sweet basil
⅓ cup whole wheat pastry
   flour
⅔ cup corn meal

Beat the eggs two seconds in the blender, add water and tomato juice, oil, salt and sweet basil, whole wheat pastry flour and corn meal. Add them slowly.

Blend to a smooth batter.

Use a six-inch skillet oiled very lightly.

Pour only enough batter, using a two-ounce ladle, to

make a thin pancake, tipping pan from side to side to cover bottom of the pan.

Bake on both sides to golden brown.

Yield: about twelve tortillas.

Filling for Enchiladas

¾ cup brown rice
4 tablespoons Safflower oil
½ cup diced onions, small
¼ teaspoon Yerba Encanta
½ teaspoon oregano powder
½ teaspoon Accent
¾ teaspoon salt
¼ cup sliced green olives
1 cup diced celery
½ cup diced green pepper
½ cup diced fresh mushrooms
½ can Worthington chicken meat substitute (sliced thin)
1 cup grated Cheddar cheese

Toast rice with two tablespoons oil. When toasted, add enough hot water to cover the rice. Cover and cook slowly until tender. Saute the onions in two tablespoons of oil. Add flavorings, also celery, green pepper, and mushrooms. Cover and simmer ten minutes.

Put rice in a mixing bowl. Add all ingredients except cheese. Mix and fill the tortillas with two tablespoons to each — roll and arrange on a hot serving dish.

Top with grated cheese and serve with hot Tomato Sauce (see Sauces).

Baked Eggplant with Tomato Sauce

1 eggplant — 1½ pound unpeeled
2 eggs
¼ cup milk
1 cup bread crumbs
½ cup whole wheat flour
½ cup cornmeal
1 teaspoon mixed herbs (sweet basil, tarragon, oregano)
1 teaspoon sea salt
1 teaspoon Accent
½ teaspoon red paprika
½ teaspoon chopped garlic

58

Wash and slice the eggplant one-half inch thick. Beat the eggs in a bowl, adding a little milk.

Mix all the dry ingredients and seasonings.

Dip the sliced eggplant first in the egg-milk mixture, then in crumb mixture on both sides. Arrange the slices in a well-oiled baking pan. Pour 1 cup water into the pan. Cover with the following sauce:

1 cup chopped onions
1 cup celery
½ cup diced green pepper
½ teaspoon vegetized salt
½ teaspoon Vegex
1½ cups water

5 cups tomato juice
5 tablespoons whole wheat flour
¼ cup lemon juice
4 tablespoons brown sugar
1 dash cayenne (red pepper)

Saute onions, celery, and green pepper. Season with salt and Vegex. Pour on ½ cup water and simmer 10 minutes. In a 1½ quart saucepan, boil tomato juice. Make a smooth paste, using whole wheat flour and water. Pour into the boiling tomato juice and stir until thickened. Fold in sauteed vegetables and ¼ cup lemon juice (or according to taste) and 4 tablespoons brown sugar. Boil slowly 2 minutes. Pour half of the sauce on the eggplant: the other half is to be used hot at serving time.

Cover and bake one hour in moderate oven at 300 degrees.

Baked Squash

¾ pound yellow summer squash
¾ pound zucchini
1 tablespoon salt
1 cup chopped onions
6 tablespoons margarine
1 cup chopped celery

1 teaspoon Accent
3 eggs
1 cup milk
½ cup chopped parsley
1 cup Rusket crumbs
2 tablespoons brown sugar

Wash and grate the squash, salt and cover. Let stand for ½ hour. Meantime saute the onions in two table-spoons melted margarine. Add celery, Accent, and mix well.

Squeeze all the excess juice off the salted squash. Combine with onions and celery mixture.

Beat the eggs and also add milk, 1 tablespoon sugar, and parsley.

Mix the ingredients well. Fold into an eight-by-nine inch buttered (or margarined) baking dish and top with the Rusket crumbs, moistened with two tablespoons of margarine, a little salt and sugar.

Bake in moderate oven — 275 or 300 degrees for ¾ hour to 1 hour until set.

Baked Rice, Number 2

1 cup brown rice	3 eggs, well beaten
2 tablespoons Safflower oil	1 small can of your
3 cups hot water	favorite meat substitute
½ cup chopped onions	

Toast the rice in one tablespoon oil. Add water and boil slowly until tender.

Saute the onions in one tablespoon oil. Add:

1 cup diced celery	½ teaspoon sea salt
20 green olives, chopped	½ teaspoon Accent
½ cup chopped green pepper	½ teaspoon sweet basil and marjoram
2 tablespoons chopped pimiento	¼ stick margarine (Sweet basil and marjoram
½ cup shredded zucchini	should be pulverized
½ teaspoon Vegex	between your palms.)

Beat the eggs. Dice the meat substitute. Fold in rice and blend well.

Dot with margarine, cover, and bake in oiled eight-by-nine inch baking dish for one hour at 300 degrees.

Baked Macaroni and Cheese

1 package soy and whole wheat macaroni (8 ounces)
2½ cups skim milk
2 tablespoons whole wheat flour
2 cups grated Cheddar cheese

1 tablespoon brown sugar
½ stick Safflower margarine
¾ cup Rusket crumbs
Red paprika

Cook macaroni in salted water until tender. Drain and wash through well with cold water. Place macaroni in a greased eight-by-nine inch baking dish.

Boil 2 cups of skim milk. Make thickening from the ½ cup milk and flour. Pour in boiling milk, stirring constantly for 1 minute. Add 1 cup grated cheese and the sugar. Mix and pour on macaroni. Sprinkle remaining cheese on top.

Melt margarine in a sauce pan. Mix in Rusket crumbs, spread over macaroni and cheese. Sprinkle lightly with red paprika.

Bake in 350 degree oven for 35-40 minutes until set and crumbs are golden brown.

Lima Bean Loaf

1½ cups large lima beans
½ cup chopped onions
2 tablespoons Safflower oil

1 teaspoon Vegex
1 cup chopped celery
1 teaspoon salt

Cook the lima beans until tender and grind in a coarse food grinder. Saute the onions in the oil. Add Vegex, celery, and salt. Mix well and add to the ground lima beans. Then add:

1 cup bread crumbs
1 cup ground pecans
2 eggs, well beaten
½ cup milk

1 teaspoon Accent
1 clove garlic, chopped
½ teaspoon thyme
1 tablespoon parsley

Mix and bake in an eight-by-nine inch baking dish for 1 hour at 300 degrees.

Serve with your favorite sauce.

Baked Spinach

1 pound of spinach	2 tablespoons Safflower oil
1 cup finely chopped onions	

Wash and chop the spinach fine. Cook one minute and drain. Saute the onions in the Safflower oil. Add to onions:

1½ cups finely chopped celery	1 clove garlic, pressed or chopped
1 teaspoon Savorex	1 teaspoon Accent
½ teaspoon salt	

Beat 4 eggs well, then add:

2 cups milk	Onion mixture
Spinach	1 cup rolled oats

Blend well. Pour in a well-oiled baking dish about eight-by-nine inch size. Cover the top with:

1 cup grated Cheddar
cheese

Bake in moderate oven at 300 degrees for one hour or until set.

½ cup finely chopped onions

2 tablespoons Safflower oil

Saute the onions. Add:

1 cup finely chopped celery
¾ cup grated jikima or celery root
½ cup diced fresh mushrooms
¼ cup chopped parsley

1 teaspoon vegetable broth powder
1 teaspoon Accent
1 teaspoon vegetized salt
½ teaspoon Vegex
½ teaspoon yeast powder

Grind separately:

1 small can or 1 cup Nuteena

½ cup cashew nuts

Pulverize 1 teaspoon sweet basil between your palms. Beat two eggs and mix well with other ingredients. Mix in one cup Rusket crumbs and 1 cup whole cashew nuts.

Bake in well-oiled eight-by-nine inch pan one hour at 275 degrees.

Protein Patties on Rice Pilaf

1 cup brown rice
3 cups water
1 cup chopped onions
1 cup chopped celery
¾ cup chopped fresh mushrooms

1 clove garlic
1 teaspoon Savita
1 teaspoon salt
½ teaspoon Accent

Boil rice in water. Saute onion, celery, mushrooms, garlic. Add Savita, salt, Accent. Add ⅓ of the sauteed vegetables to rice.

Use the rest of the sauteed vegetables and add:

1 small can or 2 cups burger, ground
2 tablespoons Torumel yeast
½ cup ground walnuts
4 eggs, well beaten
2 tablespoons chopped pimiento

2 tablespoons skim milk powder
4 tablespoons Safflower oil
1 teaspoon thyme
1 tablespoon sweet basil
½ cup crumbs

Make small patties and line them in a well-oiled covered baking dish. Add 1 cup of water.

Cover and bake 30 minutes at 300 degrees.

Put a scoop of rice on plate, place patty on top, cover it with Brown Gravy (see Sauces) and sprinkle with chopped parsley.

Baked Spinach Deluxe

1 pound spinach
1 cup finely chopped onions
Safflower oil
1½ cups finely chopped celery
1 cup grated celery root or jikima
1 cup water
2 cups milk
4 eggs, well beaten
½ cup chopped parsley
1 cup grated mild Cheddar cheese

1 cup ground cashew nuts
1 cup raw rolled oats
1 cup Rusket crumbs or flakes
1 teaspoon poultry seasoning
1 clove garlic, chopped finely
1 teaspoon Accent
1 teaspoon sweet basil
1 teaspoon sea salt

Wash spinach and drop in boiling water for a minute. Turn it, and it should be wilted. Drain and chop not too fine.

Saute onions in a well-oiled (use Safflower oil) skillet. Add celery, jikima or celery root, and pour on 1 cup water. Cover and simmer 5 minutes.

In a mixing bowl pour milk, eggs, spinach, parsley; mix well. Add the onion mixture and remaining ingredients.

Mix and bake in oiled eight-by-fourteen inch baking dish until set (about 1 hour) in 300 degree oven.

Zucchini Casserole

¾ cup buckwheat groats	3 eggs, well beaten
3 tablespoons Safflower oil	1 cup grated Cheddar
1½ cups hot water	cheese
½ cup chopped onions	

Toast buckwheat in ½ of the oil by stirring three minutes. Add 1½ cups hot water, simmer three minutes, cover and set aside.

Saute onions in the other half of the oil. Mix in:

½ teaspoon sea salt	½ teaspoon Accent
½ teaspoon Vegex	½ teaspoon rosemary

(Rosemary should be pulverized between your palms.)

1 pound zucchini, sliced	½ cup chopped celery
1 small can or 1 cup Vegeburger, cut	

Beat the eggs in a mixing bowl, fold in buckwheat, zucchini, and onion mixture. Add Vegeburger with the mixture. Pour into an eight-by-nine inch baking dish. Dot with margarine and sprinkle the cheese on top. Cover and bake one hour at 275 degrees.

⅓ cup chopped onions
1 tablespoon Safflower oil
1 can Sunnydale burger
  or other brand
1 cup ground almonds
1 cup chopped celery
½ cup chopped green
  pepper
1 cup shredded carrots

¾ cup rolled oats
2 eggs, well beaten
½ cup milk
½ teaspoon Accent
1 tablespoon chopped
  parsley
1 teaspoon sweet basil
½ teaspoon sea salt

Saute the onions in the oil. Combine with all ingredients and bake in oiled eight-by-nine inch baking dish until set, about 50-55 minutes in 300 degree oven.

Baked Eggplant Casserole

1½ pound eggplant
1 cup diced onions
Safflower oil
1 teaspoon sea salt
1 tablespoon mixed herbs
1 teaspoon Accent
1 cup diced celery
1 cup diced green
  pepper
1 clove garlic, chopped
  or pressed
3 eggs

2 cups milk
3 tablespoons margarine
1 cup bread crumbs
1 tablespoon sugar
1 cup grated Cheddar
  cheese
½ cup chopped
  mushrooms
¼ teaspoon Vegex
½ cup rolled oats
  (uncooked)

Wash the diced unpeeled eggplant. Drop into boiling water for one minute and drain.

Saute the onions in a well-oiled skillet. Mix in salt, herbs, Accent, celery, green peppers, garlic, mushrooms, and Vegex.

Beat the eggs and milk in a bowl, add oats.

Place the eggplant in an eight-by-nine inch oiled baking dish. Pour the vegetables and milk-egg mixture over it. Melt the margarine and mix in bread crumbs and sugar. Cover the top, first with the grated cheese, and then sprinkle with crumbs.

Cover and bake approximately one hour in a moderate oven at 275 degrees, or until set.

Protein Balls with Soy Spaghetti

½ cup chopped onions
¾ cup chopped green pepper
½ cup chopped mushrooms

1 clove garlic, chopped
1 can or two cups Vegeburger
6 ounces soy spaghetti
Grated cheese

Saute the onions, green peppers, mushrooms, garlic. Grind these ingredients with the Vegeburger. Put in the mixing bowl. Then add:

3 tablespoons oil
1½ cups whole wheat crumbs
½ cup skim milk powder
1 tablespoon Brewer's yeast

½ cup ground Brazil nuts
2 eggs
1 teaspoon vegetized salt
½ teaspoon Accent
1 tablespoon tarragon
1 tablespoon sweet basil

Mix well. Make little balls.

Place in well-oiled baking dish, add a cup of water and cover.

Bake ½ hour at 300 degrees.

Boil spaghetti according to instructions on the package. Place the balls on top of the spaghetti. Cover with Tomato Sauce (see Sauces) and top with your favorite grated cheese.

½ cup finely sliced avocado

2 tablespoons chopped scallions

½ hard-boiled egg, shredded

Dash of Accent

¼ teaspoon vegetized salt

Dash of cayenne pepper

Mix above ingredients. Prepare 2 slices of golden brown toast. Spread the toast with Lecinaise. Spread mixture on toast, add:

Large slice of tomato

Large slice of Cheddar cheese

Alfalfa sprouts

Cut in 4 pieces — it is a good snack.

Breaded Cutlet

½ cup chopped onions

2 tablespoons Safflower oil

½ teaspoon Vegex

½ cup chopped celery

½ cup chopped green pepper

1 Number 2 can meat substitute

2 eggs, well beaten

1 cup bread crumbs

½ teaspoon Accent

Saute the onions, add Vegex, celery, and green pepper. Grind the meat substitute together with the onion mixture in a coarse food grinder. Add eggs, 1 cup bread crumbs, and Accent. Then form patties.

Combine:

¾ cup bread crumbs

¼ cup corn meal

¼ teaspoon sea salt

¼ teaspoon sweet basil

Then beat:

1 egg   ½ cup milk

Dip patties into mixtures on both sides, first into the egg and milk, then into the crumb mixture.

Brown lightly on both sides in a well-oiled heavy skillet.

Serve with Mushroom Sauce (see Sauces).

Stuffed Eggplant

2 eggplants — ¾ pound   1 cup chopped onions
each   2 tablespoons Safflower oil

Bake the eggplants whole until fairly well done. Saute the onions in oil and add:

½ teaspoon Vegex   ½ cup peeled and diced
½ teaspoon sea salt   tomatoes
1 tablespoon brown sugar   ½ cup chopped
1 cup chopped green   mushrooms
  peppers   4 cups Tomato Sauce
1 cup chopped celery

Simmer 10 minutes. Cut the eggplants in half, scoop out the centers and chop. Mix in onion mixture and stuff the shells.

Arrange the stuffed shells in a baking dish, top with 2 cups of Tomato Sauce (see Sauces). Pour 1 cup water on bottom of the baking dish to prevent burning of the eggplant. Use the rest of the tomato sauce when serving.

Cover and bake in 350 degree oven for 25 minutes.

Celery and Pecan Loaf

¾ cup finely chopped onions

2 tablespoons Safflower oil

½ teaspoon Savita

2 cups finely chopped celery

1 cup chopped mushrooms

1 cup coarsely chopped pecans

1¼ cups Rusket crumbs

1 cup milk

2 eggs, well beaten

2 tablespoons Safflower margarine

½ teaspoon sea salt

½ teaspoon sweet basil

½ teaspoon Accent

Saute onions in the oil, add Savita. Mix well and blend all ingredients in order into a mixing bowl.

Bake in oiled eight-by-nine inch baking dish at 300 degrees for 45 minutes until set.

Serve with Country Gravy (see Sauces).

Protein Roast

½ cup chopped onions

2 tablespoons Safflower oil

1 teaspoon Savita paste

1 teaspoon sea salt

½ teaspoon Accent

½ cup diced celery

½ cup sliced fresh mushrooms

½ cup chopped green pepper

1 clove garlic, chopped

½ cup grated raw yams

1 small can Proteena (a meat substitute)

¾ cup Brazil nuts, ground

2 eggs, beaten

½ cup skim milk powder

1 cup rolled oats

1 teaspoon sweet basil

2 tablespoons wheat germ

2 tablespoons sesame seeds

Saute onions in oil. Add Savita, salt, Accent, celery, mushrooms, pepper, garlic, and yams. Simmer 15 minutes. Grind the Proteena and nuts. Add vegetables. Put in a mixing bowl, add the beaten eggs, skim milk powder (dissolved in 1/3 cup water), oats, and sweet basil. Pour into a well-oiled eight-by-nine inch baking dish. Sprinkle sesame seeds, wheat germ on top.

Bake 45 - 55 minutes at 275 degrees, until set.

Corn Meal Mush

3/4 cup yellow corn meal
3/4 cup cold water
2 cups boiling water
1/4 teaspoon sea salt

1/4 cup black manukka raisins (washed and dried)
2 tablespoons butter

Blend meal with cold water; add to boiling water and salt. Stir. Boil until it begins to thicken. Set in double boiler, add raisins, cover, let steam for 25 minutes, add butter. Serve with milk and honey.

Steamed Millet with Herbs

½ cup chopped onions
2 tablespoons Safflower oil
½ cup chopped green
  pepper
1 teaspoon salt
½ teaspoon Accent
½ cup warm water

1 cup millet
2 cups water
¼ stick Safflower
  margarine
1 tablespoon tarragon
  leaves
1 tablespoon sweet basil

Saute the onions in the oil, add green pepper, salt, and Accent. Pour on ½ cup water, simmer 5 minutes.

Cook the millet in the 2 cups of water until tender and add margarine. Mix in onion, green pepper mixture, and rub the tarragon and sweet basil between your palms over mixture.

Cover and simmer 2 more minutes.

Steamed Broccoli

2 tablespoons margarine
½ cup finely chopped
  onions
3 cups shredded
  broccoli

½ teaspoon vegetized salt
½ teaspoon Accent
1 teaspoon mixed herbs
¼ cup water

Use a heavy skillet with an airtight lid. Melt the margarine in the skillet. Add the onions, broccoli, salt, Accent, mixed herbs. Stir and add water. Keep it on lowest flame possible for 10 minutes or more. Try this method with cauliflower.

½ pound young okra   ½ cup chopped onions
1 cup water   2 tablespoons Safflower oil
½ cup lemon juice

Wash and cut off stems of okra. Bring to a boil 1 cup
of water and ½ cup lemon juice. Drop the cut okra into
boiling water and lemon juice for 2 minutes. Cover and
let stand.

Saute the onions in oil and add:

1 cup diced celery   ¾ cup diced tomatoes
½ cup chopped green   ½ clove garlic, chopped
   peppers

Simmer until vegetables are tender. Drain okra and
add to mixture. Thicken with:

3 tablespoons whole wheat   ⅓ cup water
   flour

Add:

½ teaspoon salt   ½ teaspoon sweet basil
½ teaspoon Accent

Sweeten to taste.
Makes 4 servings.

Steamed Buckwheat Groats

1 cup buckwheat   ½ teaspoon salt
4 tablespoons Safflower oil   ½ teaspoon Vegex
1 cup finely chopped   ½ teaspoon Accent
   onions

Toast buckwheat in half of the oil for five minutes.
Add hot water just to cover. Boil one minute. Put the
lid on and turn off the fire. Brown onions in remaining

oil, add salt, Vegex, Accent, and mix in the cooked buckwheat.

Serve hot, plain or with mushroom sauce. Makes 3 servings.

Suggestion: Use the same method with millet or rice, only pour in a little more water and cook longer.

Brown Rice

1 cup natural brown rice	¼ teaspoon sea salt
3 cups boiling water	

Wash the rice thoroughly. Add water and salt. Let simmer until the rice is tender — about 1 hour. Put aside, leave cover on for 15 minutes. Rice will steam up and be fluffy.

If you use double boiler, cooking time is 1½ hours. Set aside 15 minutes. Rice will stay firm.

Pickled Beets

6 medium sized beets	3 tablespoons brown sugar
1 Bermuda onion	½ teaspoon salt
½ cup lemon juice	

Wash and cook the beets until tender, strain and save all the liquid. Slice the beets thinly, also the onion. Mix in remaining ingredients.

Keep in refrigerator 3-4 hours before serving.

A very good side dish with any roast.

Soya Beans — Vegetable

1/4 cup chopped onions
1 tablespoon Safflower margarine
1/4 teaspoon Vegex
1 Number 2 can soya beans

1/4 cup chopped green peppers
1/2 teaspoon Accent

Saute the onions in the margarine. Add Vegex and mix. Add remaining ingredients and simmer 2 minutes.
Serve with any roast. Makes 4 servings.

Yellow Summer Squash or Butter Squash

1 pound squash
1/2 cup onions
1 cup water
1/2 teaspoon vegetized salt
2 tablespoons lemon juice

2 tablespoons brown sugar
1 tablespoon chopped dill weed
Yogurt

Wash and dice the squash. Cook it slowly with the onions in the water. Add remaining ingredients.
Serve hot or cold with yogurt.
Makes 3 servings.

Kohlrabi

8 small kohlrabi
1/4 cup cold water
2 tablespoons Safflower oil
2 tablespoons unbleached flour

1/2 teaspoon salt
2 tablespoons sugar
1/2 teaspoon vegetized salt

Peel and cut kohlrabi in Julienne style. Cover barely with water in sauce pan, add salt, and cook until tender. Heat the oil and brown flour lightly, adding 1/4 cup cold water. Mix and blend into the kohlrabi. Simmer 2 minutes and add sugar.
Serve as a side dish. Makes 4 servings.

Parsleyed Lyonnaise Potatoes

1 pound potatoes, cooked in jackets
½ cup chopped onions
2 tablespoons Safflower oil
1 teaspoon red paprika (Spanish sweet)
½ teaspoon salt
½ teaspoon Accent
½ cup warm water
2 tablespoons chopped parsley
Small piece garlic, finely chopped

Peel and dice the potatoes. Saute the onions in the oil, add paprika, salt, Accent, garlic and diced potatoes. Pour over ½ cup warm water. Cover and let steam thoroughly on very low flame about 15 minutes.

Serve with chopped parsley.

Zucchini Steamed with Oil and Garlic

1 pound zucchini
⅓ cup chopped onion
2 teaspoons Safflower oil

Select young zucchini and cut into inch-long pieces. Brown onions in Safflower oil and add:

1 teaspoon vegetized salt
½ teaspoon Accent
1 large clove garlic, chopped

Simmer 5 minutes, add zucchini, simmer 15 minutes. Keep covered all the time. Turn off heat. Then add:

½ cup chopped parsley
1½ tablespoons olive oil
2 tablespoons lemon juice
1 teaspoon sugar, or sugar to taste

Let stand for a few more minutes, and you have a wonderful vegetable dish.

2 bunches young beet
  leaves
1 cup finely chopped
  onions
2 tablespoons Safflower oil
½ teaspoon Vegex
½ teaspoon chopped
  garlic
1 teaspoon salt
1 teaspoon red paprika
1 bay leaf
½ teaspoon Accent
1 cup finely chopped
  celery
1 cup chopped green
  pepper
3 tomatoes
2 tablespoons whole wheat
  pastry flour
½ cup water
1 tablespoon sugar

Cut beet leaves into medium sized pieces and drop into boiling water for a minute. Drain. Brown the onions in oil and add Vegex and all flavoring. Mix well and combine with celery, green pepper, beet leaves. Peel the tomatoes, dice and add to the mixture. Simmer slowly for ½ hour. Make a smooth paste from the water and flour and mix into the vegetables. Boil for two minutes, stirring well. Add sugar and serve.

Turnips and Apples

5 small turnips
1 cup water
3 medium apples
Salt
1 tablespoon lemon juice
2 tablespoons brown sugar

Wash and wedge the turnips. Simmer in water until half done. Also wedge apples and simmer together until tender. Flavor with a dash of salt, lemon juice and sugar. Serve with the Kasha Balls or roast.

Parsleyed Potatoes

3 good size potatoes
¼ stick margarine
1 teaspoon vegetized salt
½ teaspoon Accent

2 tablespoons chopped
  parsley
½ teaspoon marjoram

Boil and peel the potatoes — cut crosswise into slices Arrange in a well-oiled baking dish. Melt the margarine and sprinkle over potatoes with the salt and Accent. Top with the parsley and marjoram.

Bake in moderate oven until golden brown at 300 degrees.

Makes 4 servings.

Kale

½ pound kale
½ cup chopped onions
1 clove garlic, chopped
1½ cups diced potatoes
1½ cups water

3 tablespoons Safflower oil
2 tablespoons whole wheat
  flour
1 teaspoon salt
Dash of black pepper

Wash and cut the kale up small. Put it in a casserole, and add onions, garlic, and diced potatoes. Cook until tender in 1 cup water.

Heat the oil, add flour and brown very lightly. Pour on ½ cup of water, bring to a boil, stirring constantly, and add to the kale.

Season with salt and black pepper.

Makes 4-6 servings.

String Beans — Hungarian Style

1 pound string beans or
  pole beans
½ cup chopped onions

2 tablespoons margarine
½ teaspoon salt
2 cups water

79

Wash and cut the beans — if pole beans, cut cross-wise; if string beans, cut length wise. Saute the onions in the margarine. Put the cut beans and salt in the sauteed onions. Cover and cook until tender in 2 cups of water.

Remove from fire and mix in:

4 tablespoons lemon juice   2 egg yolks, beaten
3 tablespoons brown sugar

You can serve it hot or cold. Makes 4-5 servings.

Creamed Spinach

¾ pound spinach, 1 bunch   ½ teaspoon Accent
2 tablespoons margarine   1 teaspoon sea salt
2 tablespoons whole wheat   ½ cup water
  flour   2 eggs
1 clove garlic, finely
  chopped

Wash and cook the spinach just 1 minute, drain and chop finely. Mix margarine and flour and brown very lightly. Put in spinach, garlic, Accent, and salt. Mix and pour on water.

Bring up to a boil and if it is too thick use a little more water. Remove from fire and beat in 2 eggs.

Serve with melted margarine on top. Makes 4-5 servings.

String Beans Deluxe

1 small can seeded sour   3 tablespoons flour
  cherries   ½ cup cold water
2 cups cut string beans

Strain juice from sour cherries. Simmer the beans with the juice and ½ cup water. If necessary, add a little water when done and add thickening of flour and water. Then add:

Sour cherries
3 tablespoons lemon juice
Little bit of grated lemon rind

Sugar to taste
Salt to taste

It is very colorful to serve.
In the summertime you can serve this cold with yogurt or sour cream, leaving out the lemon juice.

Steamed Green Leaves

½ cup chopped onions
½ cup chopped celery
½ cup chopped green peppers
½ cup chopped mushrooms
1 clove garlic, chopped
3 tablespoons oil
1 cup tomato juice
1 cup diced peeled tomatoes
2 cups cut-up pieces Swiss chard

2 cups cut-up pieces of beet tops
2 cups cut-up pieces of mustard greens
1 tablespoon brown sugar
½ cup cold water
2 tablespoons brown rice flour
¾ teaspoon sea salt
½ teaspoon Accent
½ teaspoon Yerba Encanta
¼ cup chopped parsley

Saute onions, celery, green pepper, mushrooms, and garlic in oil in a good-sized pot. Add tomato juice, heat well. Then add peeled tomato, heat again.

Now add all the green leaves, covered with brown sugar. Simmer 15-20 minutes until boiling.

Form thickening: Mix water with rice flour. Add salt, Accent, Yerba Encanta, and parsley, and it is ready to serve.

1 cup dry lentils	3 tablespoons lemon juice
3 cups water	2 tablespoons brown sugar
1 tablespoon chopped onions	½ teaspoon sea salt

Cook the lentils in 3 cups of water with the onions. When tender, add remaining ingredients and simmer 2 minutes.

Serve hot as a side dish. Makes 4 servings.

Homemade Horseradish
(Easy to Make)

2 cups unpeeled finely
  shredded turnips
½ cup finely shredded
  horseradish

1 teaspoon sea salt
½ cup lemon juice
4 tablespoons brown sugar

Wash turnips. Peel and wash horseradish. Shred on your salad maker using the finest shredder. Put in a small bowl and mix in the salt. Cover and let stand for ½ hour. Add lemon juice and sugar. Put in a jar and keep in the refrigerator.

Horseradish Sauce

Make it from your soup, using thickening (see Brown Gravy Deluxe). Take a good brand of horseradish and use according to your taste. Add 2 tablespoons fresh lemon juice, sugar and salt. This is wonderful with roasts.

Celery Root Sauce

¼ cup onions
2 tablespoons Safflower oil
1 cup diced celery root
3 cups water
3 tablespoons whole wheat
  flour

½ cup water
1 tablespoon brown sugar
½ teaspoon sea salt
1 teaspoon Accent

Saute the onions in the oil. Add celery root and 3 cups water. Cook until tender.
Make a thickening using the ½ cup water and flour.

Add to the cooked celery and let it boil until it is the desired thickness. Add remaining ingredients.

It is a tasty sauce to use with any roast.

Cheese Sauce

¼ cup flour	Accent
½ cup water	Salt
1½ cups milk	
½ cup shredded Cheddar cheese	

Use a double boiler and make a white sauce, using flour and water. Boil milk. Add white sauce slowly. Simmer two minutes. Add shredded Cheddar cheese, a little Accent, and salt to taste. Simmer until smooth.

Brown Gravy Deluxe

By now you know how to make delicious, tasty soup. Now I will tell you how to make a good gravy for when you decide to serve gravy with your meal.

Make 1 cup or 1½ cups more of your soup. When your soup is flavored and ready to serve, strain and take as much as you need.

Now you have the soup, put in a pot and heat. Take about 2 tablespoons of flour and ⅓ cup cold water to make the thickening and add it to the gravy.

Maybe you would like to add a little vegetized salt and Yerba Encanta or a little Vegex or Savita for flavor and color.

Tomato Sauce

¼ cup chopped onions
1 tablespoon Safflower oil
½ teaspoon Vegex
1 clove garlic, pressed
½ teaspoon Accent
2 tablespoons sugar
½ teaspoon sweet basil
¼ cup lemon juice
½ teaspoon sea salt
Dash of red paprika
Dash of cayenne pepper
½ cup chopped celery
½ cup chopped green
 pepper
½ cup water
3 tablespoons flour
⅔ cup water
3 cups tomato juice

Saute the onions in oil. Add Vegex, seasonings, cut vegetables, and one-half cup water. Simmer until tender. Make a thickening from the flour and water. Boil tomato juice, add thickening, then add onion mixture.

Serve hot on roast or stuffed cabbage.

Brown Gravy

½ cup whole wheat flour
4 tablespoons Safflower oil
1½ cups cold water
1 tablespoon Savita
1 teaspoon mixed herbs
½ teaspoon Accent
½ teaspoon vegetized salt

Brown the flour in the oil. Add water to desired thickness. Rub in herbs and add remaining ingredients. Simmer two minutes.

Serve on roast or vegetables.

Mushroom Gravy

½ cup finely diced onions
1 tablespoon Safflower oil
1 cup finely diced fresh
 mushrooms
Salt
Accent

Use the Brown Gravy for base. Saute the onions in oil. Add mushrooms, a little salt, and Accent. Add to the brown gravy.

Serve hot on roast or chop suey.

Country Gravy

5 tablespoons whole wheat pastry flour
4 tablespoons Safflower oil

2 cups skim milk
2 souplet squares
½ teaspoon sea salt

Brown the flour in the oil lightly. Add the milk slowly and stir until you get the desired thickness. Combine with remaining ingredients and mix well.

Serve hot on roast or Kasha Balls.

100% Whole Wheat Bread

1½ cakes yeast	1 tablespoon sea salt
3½ cups warm water	2 tablespoons sugar
6 cups whole wheat flour	2 tablespoons honey
½ cup Safflower oil	1 egg, beaten

Soak the yeast in one cup warm water. Sift the flour in a mixing bowl. Melt oil, salt, and sugar with 2½ cups warm water. With a wooden spoon, combine the beaten egg and the oil mixture with the sifted flour. Make a stiff dough and knead until smooth. Let rise in a warm place until double in bulk. Form two loaves and let rise again in an oiled large bread pan until light and spongy.

Bake ¾ hour in a moderate oven at 350 degrees. Before baking, brush over with water. When ready, brush over again to give a shiny top.

Corn Muffins

¾ cup sugar	¾ teaspoon salt
½ cup Safflower oil	4 teaspoons baking powder
2 eggs, beaten	1½ cups whole milk
1½ cups unbleached flour	1½ cups corn meal

Cream sugar and oil and add beaten eggs. Sift flour, salt, and baking powder. Alternate flour mixture and milk. Add corn meal.

Bake in well-oiled muffin pan about 20 minutes at 400 degrees.

Corn and Rye Bread

2 cakes yeast
2¾ cups warm water
1 cup corn meal
3 cups rye flour
5 cups unbleached flour
2 eggs

2 tablespoons honey
3 tablespoons brown sugar
2 tablespoons salt
¾ cup Safflower oil
2 cups warm milk

Soften the yeast in ¾ cup water. Pour one cup of warm water over the corn meal. Sift the rye and unbleached flour in a mixing bowl. Beat the eggs and add to the flour. Mix the honey, sugar, salt, and oil into the yeast when dissolved and then add to the flour along with the remaining one cup of warm water and warm milk.

Make a fairly soft dough, knead until smooth, dipping your hand in warm water frequently to avoid sticking. Flour the dough and cover with a tea towel and keep in a warm place. When it has raised and doubled in size, pour it on a floured board, divide into four loaves and place in oiled baking loaf pans.

Let it rise again about one hour and bake in a moderate oven at 350 degrees for 45 minutes until you get a nice light brown crust. Brush loaves with warm water *before* and after baking.

Whole Grain Bread

2 cakes yeast
5 cups warm water
3 cups rye flour
½ cup Safflower oil
3 tablespoons salt

3 tablespoons sugar
2 eggs
6 cups whole wheat flour
3 tablespoons honey

Soak the yeast in 1 cup warm water. Sift flour in a gallon size mixing bowl. Take four cups warm water and melt in the oil, salt, sugar, and honey.

With wooden spoon, combine beaten eggs, yeast and water mixture with the flour, making a fairly stiff batter.

Knead until batter is smooth. If you use an electric mixer, let the batter be a little harder. Sprinkle with flour and let it rise until it doubles in bulk. Form four loaves and arrange in well-oiled loaf pans. Let rise in pan until it almost reaches rim.

Brush with water and bake ¾ hour at 350 degrees. When baked, brush over again with clear water for shiny top.

Holy Day Twist

2 cakes yeast	1½ teaspoons sea salt
1 cup warm water	4 tablespoons brown sugar
4 cups unbleached flour	1 whole egg, beaten
2 cups whole wheat flour	4 egg yolks
3 cups milk	
1 stick of Safflower margarine	

Soak the yeast in one cup of warm water. Sift the flour in a mixing bowl. Heat the milk and melt the margarine, salt, and sugar. Combine one whole beaten egg, and 2 yolks, yeast, and the milk mixture with the flour, with a wooden spoon.

Make a rather stiff dough, but not too hard to knead. Work until smooth. Sprinkle the top with unbleached flour. Let rise until double in bulk. Place on a floured board. Cut it in six pieces. Roll it two inches thick and a little longer than the loaf pan. Take three and braid. Put it in oiled loaf pans.

Let rise again. Brush with egg yolk.

Bake in 300 degree oven for 15 minutes; then 350 degree oven for 30 minutes. It will rise in the oven, so brush over with egg yolk to get even color.

Yield: two large twist loaves.

Coffee Cake

2 cups whole wheat flour
1 teaspoon sea salt
2½ teaspoons baking powder
1 stick Safflower margarine

1 cup brown sugar
1 egg, well beaten
1 cup milk
2 teaspoons vanilla

Measure flour into a mixing bowl. Add salt and baking powder and mix. Melt the margarine and add all the ingredients in order. Mix well. Pour the batter into a greased eight-by-nine inch baking dish, and combine:

½ stick margarine, melted
3 tablespoons flour

4 tablespoons sugar
1 teaspoon cinnamon

Sprinkle on top and bake 45 minutes in a moderate oven, 325 degrees.

Blueberry Muffins

4 rounded tablespoons brown sugar
½ cup Safflower oil
1 egg, well beaten
2 cups unbleached flour

5 teaspoons baking powder
½ teaspoon sea salt
1½ cups milk
1 small can blueberries
¼ cup whole wheat flour

Cream sugar and oil. Add beaten egg. Add sifted unbleached flour, baking powder, and salt. Alternate milk with flour mixture.

Drain berries and fold into whole wheat flour and combine with the mixture and let stand ten minutes.

Fill greased muffin pans ¾ full and bake in hot oven for 25 minutes at 375 degrees.

3 cups whole wheat flour
1 cake of yeast or 1
  envelope of dry yeast
¾ cup of lukewarm water
1 stick Safflower
  margarine

2 tablespoons brown sugar
1 teaspoon sea salt
1¼ cups warm milk
2 tablespoons sour cream
1 whole egg

Measure the flour into a mixing bowl. Soak the yeast in the warm water. Put margarine, sugar, and salt into the warm milk. When dissolved, add to the flour. Also add the soaked yeast, sour cream, and egg. Make a fairly soft dough and work it until it gets smooth.

If you are using electric mixer, leave the dough a little harder.

Let is rise until bulk is doubled.

½ stick margarine, melted
2 cups brown sugar
2 teaspoons cinnamon

½ cup raisins
2 egg yolks

Roll the dough out on a floured board about ½ inch thick, then brush with the melted margarine, and sprinkle heavily with the mixture of sugar and cinnamon. Top with the raisins.

Roll the dough tightly, pulling it to better handling. Then cut crosswise into 12 pieces and arrange, cut side up, in an eight-by-fourteen inch baking dish, three in a row. Press it a little and let it rise about ½ hour and brush with egg yolk. Bake in 300 degree oven for 15-20 minutes.

Date and Nut Horns

2 eggs	¼ teaspoon salt
1½ cups brown sugar	2 teaspoons vanilla
1½ cups coarsely chopped walnuts	¼ teaspoon cloves
	½ teaspoon baking soda
1 cup chopped dates	1 cup shredded coconut
¾ cup Rusket crumbs	Confectioners' sugar

Beat the eggs; add sugar and beat well. Add all the ingredients in order except the coconut and confectioners' sugar.

Make 24 balls and roll in the coconut, shaping into little horns.

Arrange on a floured cookie sheet and bake 30 minutes in a moderate 325 degree oven. Dust with confectioners' sugar.

Linser Cookies

3 sticks Safflower margarine	1 teaspoon salt
	½ cup lemon juice
3 cups brown sugar	1 lemon rind, grated
4 eggs	2 beaten egg whites
4-5 cups whole wheat or unbleached flour	1 cup ground walnuts
	¾ cup brown sugar
1 teaspoon baking powder	

Cream the margarine with the sugar, add eggs one by one, beat well after each addition. Add the flour, sifted with baking powder, salt, then lemon juice and rind. Make a fairly soft dough.

Roll out half of the dough at a time on a floured board to one-inch thickness. Make stars or hearts with a cookie cutter, or any design cutter you have. Brush with lightly

93

beaten egg whites and sprinkle the tops with ground walnuts and brown sugar.

Arrange the cookies on a floured cookie sheet and bake to a golden brown (about 20 minutes) in a moderate 350 degree oven.

Nut and Coconut Chews

1 stick Safflower margarine	3 tablespoons brown sugar
	1 cup whole wheat flour

Cream margarine and sugar well and blend in flour. Put this dough into an eight-by-nine inch oiled baking dish. Press it well and evenly and bake at 325 degrees about 30 minutes until golden brown.

2 eggs	2 teaspoons vanilla
1¾ cups brown sugar	¼ teaspoon cinnamon
1 cup chopped walnuts	¼ teaspoon sea salt
¾ cup shredded coconut	Confectioners' sugar
½ cup chopped dates	

Beat the 2 egg yolks, add sugar and mix it well. Add chopped nuts, coconut, dates, vanilla, cinnamon, and salt.

Fold in stiffly beaten egg whites, and blend it gently.

Pour over baked mixture and return to oven for 25 minutes. Cool before cutting. Then cut into one-inch squares and dust them with confectioners' sugar.

Dates and Pecan Muffins

½ stick Safflower margarine	¼ teaspoon salt
	1½ cups skim milk
4 tablespoons brown sugar	1½ cups coarsely chopped pecans
2 eggs, well beaten	1 cup chopped dates
2½ cups whole wheat flour	
4 teaspoons baking powder	

Cream the margarine with the sugar. Add eggs, flour sifted with the baking powder, and salt. Add milk alternately with the flour. Add pecans and dates. Mix and let stand ten minutes.

Fill greased muffin pans ¾ full and bake 25 minutes in hot oven at 375 degrees.

Orange Lemon Cake

3 medium oranges
½ lemon
1¼ cups pecans
1½ cups manukka raisins
2¼ cups whole wheat
    flour
½ teaspoon sea salt
1¼ teaspoon baking soda

1½ cups brown sugar
1¼ cups non-fat milk
2 tablespoons wheat germ
1 tablespoon vanilla
1 stick Safflower
    margarine, melted
3 eggs, well beaten

Squeeze the oranges and lemon, save the juice. Grind the peel of the lemon and oranges with the pecans and raisins.

Sift flour, salt, and soda in a mixing bowl; add sugar, milk, wheat germ, and vanilla. Mix well.

Add margarine and eggs; blend well. Add the ground fruit and nut mixture and blend well.

Bake in an eight-by-twelve inch baking dish in 325 degree oven for 25 minutes, then lower the heat to 300 degrees and bake another 25 minutes.

Mix the juice with 2 tablespoons brown sugar and sprinkle on the warm cake.

Carrot Cake

1 stick Safflower margarine	1½ cups brown sugar
	3 eggs, well beaten

Cream the margarine and add the brown sugar and eggs. Mix well. Then add:

2½ cups whole wheat pastry flour	½ teaspoon baking soda
2 teaspoons baking powder	

Mix well and add:

1 cup chopped walnuts	2 teaspoons vanilla
2 cups grated raw carrots	½ teaspoon cinnamon

Blend well and bake in an oiled and floured eight-by-twelve inch baking dish in 350 degree oven for 45 minutes.

Serve with light cream.

Fruit Cake

¼ pound (1 stick) Safflower margarine	1 cup chopped dates
	1 cup coarsely chopped pecans
1 cup brown sugar	
1 egg	½ cup raisins
1½ cups whole wheat pastry flour	½ teaspoon cinnamon
	1 tablespoon vanilla
½ teaspoon sea salt	¼ teaspoon powdered cloves
2 teaspoons baking powder	
½ teaspoon baking soda	1½ cups apple sauce

Cream margarine with the sugar. Add one beaten egg. Sift 1¼ cups flour with the salt, baking powder, and baking soda. Add to the margarine, sugar and egg mixture. Dates, pecans, and raisins should be mixed with ¼ cup of flour for better handling.

Add remaining seasonings and apple sauce. Mix well.

Pour into an eight-by-nine inch well-oiled and floured pan. Bake one hour in moderate oven at 275 degrees.

Cherry Pecan Cake

8 eggs
2 cups brown sugar
1½ cups whole wheat
   pastry flour
½ teaspoon salt

3 tablespoons lemon juice
1 can pitted sour cherries
1½ cups coarsely
   chopped pecans
½ teaspoon cinnamon

Separate the eggs. Beat the yolks well. Add 1½ cups sugar. Beat until light. Add flour, sifted before measuring — also salt and lemon juice. Beat egg whites. Mix gently with the flour mixture. Pour into an eight-by-twelve inch oiled and floured baking pan.

Arrange the strained cherries on top; then sprinkle over with the pecans and a mixture of ½ cup sugar and cinnamon. Bake ¾ hour in moderate oven, 300 degrees for 15 minutes and lower to 275 degrees for 30 more minutes.

Carob and Yogurt Cake

3 eggs
1½ cups brown sugar
2½ cups of unbleached
   flour
1 teaspoon soda
1 teaspoon salt
¾ stick Safflower
   margarine

½ cup Waconia sorghum
2 teaspoons vanilla
¾ cup instant carob
   powder
1 cup yogurt

Using an electric mixer, beat the eggs, add sugar and beat well. Sift the flour, soda, and salt together. Add half the flour mixture to the egg and sugar; then margarine, sorghum, vanilla, instant carob powder, and the rest of the flour mixture. Blend in the yogurt gently with a wooden spoon.

Then pour into a greased nine-by-fourteen inch baking pan and bake for 45 minutes at 300 degrees.

Apple-Apricot Delight

3 cups thinly sliced
  apples
½ cup chopped apricots
1 cup water

½ teaspoon cinnamon
½ stick Safflower
  margarine
1 cup brown sugar

Steam apples and apricots in the 1 cup of water with the cinnamon. Arrange in an eight-by-nine inch baking dish, oiled with Safflower oil.

Cream margarine with sugar. Then add:

1½ cups rolled oats
¼ teaspoon cloves
¼ teaspoon nutmeg

¼ teaspoon sea salt
¾ cup pine nuts

Pour over apples and apricots and bake 15 minutes at 300 degrees.

Brown Rice Pudding

1 cup brown rice
2½ cups water
3 eggs

¾ cup brown sugar
¼ teaspoon nutmeg

Boil the rice in the water until tender and all the liquid has been absorbed. Cover and let stand for ½ hour after cooking, and the rice will be fluffy.

Beat the eggs well, add sugar and beat it to a lemon color. Then add:

Cooked rice
3 cups milk
½ teaspoon salt
½ cup shredded apple

1 tablespoon vanilla
2 tablespoons lemon juice
½ cup black manukka
  raisins

Mix well and pour into buttered eight-by-nine inch baking pan. Sprinkle with the nutmeg.

Bake in moderate oven at 300 degrees for 45 minutes until set.

Apricot Whip

½ cup dried apricots   2 tablespoons maple syrup
1 cup pineapple juice   ½ cup yogurt
Pinch of salt

Soak apricots overnight. Add all ingredients except yogurt, and whip in the blender. Then add yogurt and blend until thoroughly mixed.

You can use this method with prunes. Soak prunes in hot water overnight.

Fruit Pudding

To make a fine fruit pudding, take your leftover cakes, cinnamon rolls or whatever dry cake you have (about 1 pound). You can add raisin bread or soya bread.

Soak cake or bread in milk. When all the milk is absorbed, cream one stick of margarine, mix in 1½ cups brown sugar and beat in 3 eggs.

Squeeze milk out of cake, add to the egg mixture. Grate 2 medium apples, 1 cup chopped nuts (any kind), ½ cup raisins, 1 tablespoon vanilla, ½ teaspoon cinnamon, ¼ teaspoon cloves, 2 teaspoons baking powder and ½ cup Rusket crumbs. Add to the mixture of margarine, etc.

Blend well and bake in oiled eight-by-nine inch baking dish about 1 hour at 300 degrees.

Serve with Lemon Sauce.

Lemon Sauce

Boil 2 cups of water, make a smooth paste from 3 tablespoons unbleached flour and ½ cup cold water. Strain, then slowly pour into the boiling water, stirring all the time. Boil until desired thickness.

Take away from fire, add ½ cup lemon juice, pinch of salt and sugar to taste. Beat 2 egg yolks and mix into the sauce.

Apple Sauce

3 tablespoons honey	4 cups unpeeled grated
3 tablespoons lemon juice	apples (cored)
Dash of salt	

Put the honey, lemon juice, and salt in the blender. Add the grated apple 1 cup at a time and blend until smooth. Serve cold.

Pumpkin and Sweet Potato Pie

1 stick margarine	½ cup cold water
1¼ cups whole wheat	1 egg, well beaten
pastry flour	1 teaspoon brown sugar
¼ teaspoon baking	Pinch of salt
powder	

Rub margarine into flour, add remaining ingredients, and mix lightly. Let stand in refrigerator 30 minutes. Put on lightly floured board and roll out a little larger than a nine-inch pie plate. To keep from breaking, roll pie crust around the roller, and unroll in the pie pan. Press the dough to the rim of the pan, pinching with fingers to make scalloped edge. Put three sets of holes in the bottom of the crust to prevent bubbling.

Bake in 300 degree oven 10 minutes, until half done.

Prepare filling:

2 eggs   1 cup brown sugar

Beat eggs in a bowl, and mix with brown sugar, using wooden spoon. Add:

1 Number 2 can pumpkin   ½ cup light cream
  for pies   ½ teaspoon nutmeg
1½ pounds sweet potatoes,   ½ teaspoon cinnamon
  boiled, peeled and grated ¼ teaspoon cloves
                             1 teaspoon vanilla extract

Mix all ingredients well. Fill the half-baked pie shell and bake in 300 degree oven for 1 hour.
Serve with whipped cream.

To Sprout Alfalfa Seed
(The Way I Do It)

Take a big-mouthed gallon jar. Soak 3 tablespoons alfalfa seed over night. Next day, strain seeds, spread on inside of the jar. Lay the jar on its side — cover about ⅓ of the jar. Cover the jar opening with cheesecloth.

The next day, wet the seeds and strain *well:* putting strainer over mouth of jar, invert and strain.

Put cheesecloth back, always. Do this for six days and you will have the fresh sprouts ready. Wash sprouts in colander with cold water to remove seeds. Shake well. Refrigerate in plastic bag.

It is wonderful on sandwiches and salads instead of lettuce. Sprinkle on a little vegetized salt.

After using the jar, wash it well with soap powder, rinse, dry; and it is ready to use again.

Vegetable Liver Appetizer

1 cup chopped onions	2 hard-boiled eggs
2 tablespoons Safflower oil	1 small can or 1 cup
½ pound string beans	nuttose

Saute onions in the oil and let cool. Wash and cook the string beans until tender. Grind together all the ingredients. Add:

½ teaspoon vegetized salt	½ teaspoon Yerba
½ teaspoon Accent	Encanta
1 teaspoon sweet basil, rubbed in palms	

Serve cold on lettuce bed, garnished with chopped parsley.

Eggplant Appetizer

1 eggplant — 1 pound
1 cup finely diced celery
1 cup finely chopped
  onions
1 cup diced green pepper
2 cloves garlic, pressed or
  chopped

5 tablespoons lemon juice
½ teaspoon salt
¼ cup chopped pimiento
1 teaspoon brown sugar

Bake the eggplant whole; then cool and peel. Chop finely. Mix it with all the ingredients. Cool in refrigerator.

Serve on lettuce leaf with sliced tomatoes and chopped parsley.

Tomato Surprise Appetizer

4 medium tomatoes
¼ cup chopped celery
¼ cup finely chopped
  onions
¼ cup finely chopped
  olives
¼ cup chopped green
  pepper

2 hard-boiled eggs,
  shredded
2 tablespoons lemon juice
2 tablespoons Lemonaise
  or Lecinaise
1 teaspoon brown sugar

Cut tops off the tomatoes. Scrape the insides out and dice small. Mix diced tomatoes with all the ingredients. Fill the tomato shells.

Serve on crisp lettuce leaf with a sprig of parsley.

Potato Peel Broth Drink

2 cups Potato Peel Broth
  (see Soups)
2 level teaspoons Torumel
  yeast
3 level teaspoons Goodie
  high protein powder (or
  other protein powder)

2 egg yolks
Dash of nutmeg or
  paprika

Pour the broth in the blender, add yeast and protein and blend 10 seconds.

Add egg yolks and blend another 10 seconds.

If you wish to add flavor, add dash of nutmeg or paprika.

This is a wonderful high protein drink.

Potato Peel and Okra Drink

2 cups Potato Peel Broth
  (see Soups)

6 okra (very young)

Wash okra, cut in about 2 inch size pieces. Whip in the blender with broth until smooth.

Corn Milk

Here is a tasty broth which is easy to make.

2 cups fresh cut corn, or a
  small can of corn
1 quart skim milk

4 tablespoons honey
2 egg yolks
Dash of salt

Put milk and corn in the blender and run it until smooth. Strain, and then put the liquid back in the blender. Add honey, egg yolks, and salt.

Run it for a few minutes until smooth.

It is a very nourishing broth.

For refreshing drinks, here are a few quick combinations:

Papaya, pineapple and coconut milk. This should be liquified to blend the coconut.

Peach, pineapple and a little apple juice.

Mango juice with lemonade.

Boysenberry and apple juice.

For a snack:

10 ounces skim milk	1 tablespoon honey
1 medium banana	1 egg yolk
1 tablespoon blanched almonds	

Whip in blender until smooth.

SAVOR WITHOUT SALT

BOOK TWO

Vegetable Soup

½ cup chopped onion
1 cup diced carrots
1 cup diced parsnips
½ cup diced turnips

¼ chopped leeks
1 cup cut string beans
7 cups water

Cook all the vegetables in 7 cups of water until tender. Take out 1 cup of the vegetables and 1½ cups broth and put into blender. Add:

½ cup cashew nuts
½ cup chopped parsley

1 clove garlic, pressed
Dill weed or seed

Blend until smooth. Pour into the boiling soup. Serve hot with dulse powder.

Thick Vegetable Soup

¾ cup dry lima beans
8 cups water
1 cup diced parsnips
½ cup diced turnips
½ cup diced carrots
½ cup chopped onions

1 clove garlic, chopped or
    pressed
½ cup cashew nuts
Kelp powder
Dill weed
Parsley

Cook lima beans in five cups of water until almost tender, add three more cups water and the cut vegetables, cook slowly about twenty-five minutes until all vegetables are tender. Take out 1½ cups of the mixed vegetables and two cups broth, add cashew nuts, put in the blender and whip until smooth; add to the soup.

Serve with chopped dill weed and parsley. Add kelp powder to taste.

Beet Soup

6 medium beets   1 cup yogurt
8 cups water

Wash beets and cook in water until tender (save juice). Peel and shred the beets. Place in a big jar. Cover with:

½ cup lemon juice   Beet juice
½ cup brown sugar

Keep in refrigerator overnight.
Next day, put it in a blender and blend with the yogurt.
Serve cold with extra yogurt if you desire.

Green Cabbage Soup

3 cups chopped cabbage   3 cups tomato juice
½ cup chopped onions   2 tablespoons whole wheat
½ cup diced potatoes   flour
  (peeled)   ½ cup cold water
4 cups water   2 tablespoons sugar
1 tablespoon caraway   3 tablespoons lemon juice
  seeds   1 cup yogurt

Cook the cabbage, potatoes, and onions in 3 cups water for 15 minutes. Boil the caraway seeds separately in 1 cup of water for 3 minutes and set aside. Add the tomato juice to the cooked cabbage. Let it boil, and thicken with the flour mixed in the ½ cup cold water. Add sugar, lemon juice, and liquid drained from the caraway seeds to the soup. Mix it, take away from fire. Beat the yogurt smooth and mix it in the soup.

Serve immediately.

Potassium Broth

2 carrots
2 parsnips
1 whole turnip
1 green pepper
½ bunch parsley
1 tomato

1 small potato unpeeled
and halved
1 clove garlic
1 onion, halved, unpeeled
8 cups water
Kelp

Wash and cut up vegetables in big pieces. Pour on 8 cups water. Cook until vegetables are tender. Strain and season with kelp. The clear liquid may be served throughout the day. It is delicious without anything.

Mushroom Barley Soup

½ cup barley
7 cups water
1 cup diced parsnips
½ cup diced carrots
½ cup diced jikima
1 clove garlic, chopped

½ cup chopped onions
1 cup chopped
mushrooms
2 tablespoons Safflower oil
¼ cup chopped parsley
Dulse powder

Cook the barley separately in 2 cups of water until tender. Cook the vegetables, except the onions and mushrooms, in the 5 cups of water. Saute the onions in the oil, add mushrooms and saute for 3 minutes. Blend together with the cooked barley and vegetables. Season with the parsley and dulse powder.

Mock Chicken Gumbo Soup

½ cup chopped onions
½ cup diced carrots
1 cup diced parsnips
½ cup diced turnips
1 clove garlic, chopped
½ cup sliced mushrooms

7 cups water
1 cup okra, cut crosswise
½ cup cashew nuts
Parsley
Kelp powder

Cook all the vegetables together, except the okra, in 7 cups water until tender. Take out one cup vegetables and two cups of the broth, put in blender with cashew nuts and blend until smooth. Combine with the soup and the cut okra, simmer three minutes.

Serve with chopped parsley and kelp powder.

Green Lima Bean Soup

1½ cups green lima beans
½ cup chopped onions
½ cup diced parsnips
½ cup diced carrots
½ diced turnips

1 clove garlic, chopped
7 cups water
2 tablespoons whole wheat flour
½ cup cold water

Cook together all vegetables in 7 cups of water until tender. Take flour and cold water; mix to a smooth paste and stir into boiling soup. Simmer 2 minutes.

Season with:

Chopped parsley
½ tablespoon brown sugar

Dulse powder

Lentil Soup

1 cup lentils	½ cup diced parsnips
6 cups water	1 clove garlic, chopped
½ cup diced carrots	½ cup cashew nuts
½ cup diced onions	

Cook lentils in 6 cups water. Cook the vegetables separately in 2 cups water since they do not need as much cooking as the lentils. Combine together and take out 2 cups and put in the blender with cashew nuts. Blend until smooth and mix in the soup. Simmer 2 minutes, season with:

Chopped parsley	½ teaspoon kelp
½ teaspoon bacon yeast	

Serve hot.

Beet and Apple Soup

2 cups shredded beets	1 tablespoon lemon juice
2 cups diced apples	3 tablespoons yogurt or
8 cups water	sour cream
2 rounded tablespoons black manukka raisins	1 tablespoon honey

Cook beets in 5 cups water and apples in 3 cups water separately. Bring to a boil, then simmer until tender. Do not overcook. As soon as the apples boil, add the raisins. Mix lemon juice, yogurt and honey with enough broth to make it easy to whip up. Add to the cooked beets and apples.

Serve with a baked or boiled potato for a nice lunch.

1½ cups split peas
9 cups water
½ cup chopped onions
½ cup diced parsnips

½ cup diced carrots
1 clove garlic, chopped or
  pressed

Soak the peas in two cups of water overnight. Next day, put in a two-quart sauce pan and cover with 4 cups of water, add chopped onions and cook slowly until tender.

Cook the rest of the vegetables separately in 3 cups of water. Add to the cooked pea soup.

Make thickening from:

2 tablespoons whole wheat
  flour

½ cup cold water

Pour in the boiling soup. Let simmer two minutes. Season with:

Chopped parsley
¼ teaspoon bacon yeast

Kelp powder

Avocado and Egg Salad

4 Calavo avocados
Salad greens
½ cup fresh lime juice
4 hard-boiled eggs
1 tablespoon finely
    chopped onion

2 tablespoons Lecinaise
½ cup chopped pimiento
½ cup chopped parsley
1 large tomato

Wash and cut avocados in half. Arrange salad greens on a platter. Place avocado halves on them and sprinkle with lime juice. Grate the eggs in a mixing bowl. Add remaining ingredients except tomato. Mix and fill centers of avocados. Garnish with wedged tomatoes. Sprinkle with fresh parsley.

Serve with French dressing.

Waldorf Salad with Yam

1 boiled yam (¾ pound)
½ cup shredded jikima
½ cup chopped green
    pepper
1 cup diced unpeeled
    apples

½ cup chopped pecans
4 large dates, diced
3 tablespoons honey
½ cup lemon juice
3 tablespoons apple juice

Dice yam in a salad bowl.

115

Sprinkle on the jikima, green pepper, and apples with the pecans and dates. Make a mixture of the honey, lemon juice, and apple juice. Pour over the salad.

Serve cold. Makes 2-3 servings.

Vegetable Salad

1 cup chopped pecans
2 cups grated tart apples
3 cups finely shredded green cabbage
½ cup finely chopped scallions

½ cup black manukka raisins
1 tablespoon finely chopped fresh peppermint leaves

Mix well and arrange on a bed of romaine lettuce leaves in a large salad bowl.

Decorate with:

16 tomato wedges
8 carrot sticks

8 cucumber sticks

Serve with Vegetable Salad Dressing (see Salad Dressings).

Green Cabbage Salad

2 cups finely chopped
green cabbage
1 cup diced green
pepper
½ cup pimiento (red bell
pepper)

1 cup shredded jikima
Mexican root
1 cup shredded winesap
apples
½ cup ground walnuts

Mix all ingredients together in a salad bowl.

Serve with Green Cabbage Salad Dressing (see Salad
Dressings).

Grapes and Avocado Salad

1 pound seedless
Thompson grapes
1 pound ripe but firm
avocado, peeled and
diced

2 tablespoons shredded
coconut

Take off grapes from the stems, wash and arrange in a
salad bowl. Top with the diced avocado. Sprinkle with the
shredded coconut.

Serve cold with whole wheat crackers. This makes a
very tasty salad.

Chop up romaine and bronze lettuce, thinly spread on plate. In center, put one scoop of salt-free cottage cheese, circle with wedges of tomatoes (cut side should lean toward cheese). Place young cauliflower buds on one side and young broccoli buds on the other side. Slice young cucumber, placed on edges.

Fill the empty spots with young scallions and asparagus tips. Put a little yogurt over cottage cheese and top with honey.

Sprinkle the salad with chopped almonds.

Spring Salad

3 large scoops salt-free cottage cheese
½ cup yogurt
Dash of paprika
6 carrot sticks
6 celery sticks
½ cup finely chopped radishes
½ cup finely chopped green peppers
½ cup finely chopped scallions and chives

Place cottage cheese in center of plate. Top with yogurt and a dash of paprika. Surround with the carrot sticks and the celery sticks. Spread chopped mixture on top.

Colorful Tropical Salad Plate
(It's a Meal)

6 large slices Hayden
  mango
6 large slices papaya
6 half-slices pineapple
6 oranges, cut in wedges
6 dates, cut in half
2 large dried figs, cut in
  half

1 banana, sliced
½ cup watermelon balls
2 tablespoons cashew nuts
2 tablespoons shredded
  coconut

Place mango, papaya, and pineapple crosswise on plate. Fill in the empty spots with the oranges, dates, and figs. Place banana on edges. Scatter the watermelon balls for color effect. Sprinkle with cashew nuts and shredded coconut.

Serve with dressing made by mixing:

2 tablespoons honey
1 tablespoon water

3 tablespoons lemon juice

Vegetable Salad Dressing

2 eggs   ½ cup olive oil

Beat the eggs in the blender at low speed. Add the olive oil slowly, continue blending until oil has emulsified. Then add:

½ cup lemon juice   2 tablespoons chopped
1 clove garlic   dill weed
1 cup diced tomatoes   1 teaspoon kelp powder
2 tablespoons brown
  sugar

Serve cold over Vegetable Salad (see Salads).

Salad Dressing

⅓ cup lemon juice   2 egg yolks
⅓ cup apple cider vinegar   ¾ cup Safflower oil
2½ tablespoons honey

Mix lemon juice, apple cider vinegar, and honey. Start blender on low speed with egg yolks for a short minute. Add:

1 teaspoon dulse   1 teaspoon sweet basil
Small piece of garlic,   ½ teaspoon paprika
  chopped

Run blender 1½ minutes. Add the oil and run blender 1½ minutes. This will be a thin dressing.

If you want a heavier dressing, start with oil. Blender should run on low speed. Put in the oil very slowly. This will thicken. Put in all ingredients and run blender 3 more minutes.

½ cup lemon juice ½ cup brown sugar
⅓ cup cold water ¼ cup soya bean oil

Mix with Green Cabbage Salad (see Salads), and top with the following:

1 tablespoon chopped Kelp powder
  dill weed
1 tablespoon chopped
  parsley

Serve cold.

Soy Bean and Millet Roast

1 cup cooked soy beans
1 cup cooked millet
½ cup chopped onions or scallions
½ cup chopped green pepper
¾ cup chopped mushrooms
1 teaspoon oil

2 eggs
¼ stick margarine
¾ cup tomato juice
1 teaspoon fresh marjoram or sage, chopped fine
¼ cup raw sugar
Dulse or kelp

Saute onions, green peppers, mushrooms in oil for 10 minutes. Mix remaining ingredients.

Bake in well-oiled baking dish, 325 degrees about 45-50 minutes.

Baked Cauliflower with Cheese

1 pound head of cauliflower
3 cups skim milk
1 tablespoon whole wheat flour
¼ cup cold water or milk
1 cup shredded Cheddar cheese

½ teaspoon kelp
½ cup low-sodium whole wheat bread crumbs
1 tablespoon brown sugar
1 tablespoon oil
Dulse

Wash and cut the cauliflower into eight or more pieces. Place in boiling water for three minutes. Cool and arrange the cauliflower in an oiled eight-by-ten inch baking dish.

Heat the milk in a sauce pan. Make thickening of the flour (you can use juice of the cauliflower or milk). Add shredded cheese and ½ teaspoon kelp. Cook until smooth and pour it over cauliflower.

Mix bread crumbs with the sugar and 1 tablespoon oil. Sprinkle over cheese sauce. Bake at 325 degrees for 30 minutes. Sprinkle with dulse.

Chow Mein

1 cup brown rice	½ cup water chestnuts
3 cups water	(shredded raw)
½ cup carrots	½ cup sliced mushrooms
½ cup jikima or	1 cup bean sprouts
Jerusalem artichoke	(use raw)
1 cup sliced Swiss chard	¼ cup chopped parsley or
½ cup sliced onions	green pepper
½ cup fresh peas (if	Dulse or kelp
young use raw)	

Cook rice in 3 cups of water until tender. Cut the vegetables Chinese style, slanted. Cook carrots, artichoke, Swiss chard together, but jikima separately. When carrots are almost ready, drop in the onions.

Serve rice on bottom of the plate. Cover first with the cooked vegetables, peas, water chestnuts. Now spread on Mushroom Sauce (see Sauces). Top with bean sprouts and green pepper or chopped parsley. Flavor with dulse or kelp.

2 tablespoons Safflower oil
½ cup finely chopped
onions
2 cups grated jikima
2 cups grated chayote

½ cup grated carrots
1 cup chopped
mushrooms
1 cup warm water

Saute onions in the oil and add the jikima, chayote, carrots, and mushrooms. Mix well before adding water. Cover and simmer 10 minutes.

3 eggs
2 tablespoons chopped
parsley
1 cup skim milk

1 clove garlic, finely
chopped or pressed
1 cup Spanish peanuts,
ground

Beat the eggs in a mixing bowl, then add the parsley, skim milk, garlic, and Spanish peanuts. Add the onion mixture, mix well, and add:

1 cup bread crumbs
½ cup uncooked rolled
oats
1 teaspoon sweet basil,
pulverized between your
palms

Dulse (powdered) to
taste

Mix well and bake in an eight-by-nine inch oiled baking dish in moderate, 300 degree oven for 1 hour until set.

Zucchini and Rice Casserole

1 cup brown rice
3 cups water
½ cup diced onions
3 tablespoons Safflower oil
1 cup chopped Swiss
  chard
2 cups medium sliced
  zucchini
½ cup fresh thinly sliced
  mushrooms

1 clove garlic, chopped
1 teaspoon sweet basil
½ teaspoon marjoram
1 teaspoon kelp powder
2 eggs
½ cup grated unsalted
  Tillamook cheese
½ stick Safflower
  margarine

Wash the rice and cook it in 3 cups of water until tender. Set aside and cover. Saute onions in the oil. Add remaining ingredients except eggs, cheese, and margarine. Simmer together for 3 minutes. Add to cooked rice. Beat the eggs and mix in well. Pour in eight-by-nine inch baking dish. Sprinkle top with grated cheese and dot with margarine. Bake in 325 degree oven for 40-45 minutes until well set.

Baked Brown Rice

1 cup chopped onions
2 tablespoons Safflower
  oil

Saute the onions in the oil. Add:

½ cup sliced mushrooms
½ cup chopped parsley
½ cup chopped olives —
  green or black

1 clove garlic, chopped
½ teaspoon sweet basil
1 teaspoon kelp or dulse

Simmer for fifteen minutes. Fold in mixing bowl:

2 cups cooked brown rice

126

Add:

Sauteed onion mixture
1 cup skim milk
2 whole eggs, well beaten

½ stick unsalted margarine

Mix well. Pour in a well-oiled eight-by-nine inch baking dish and dot with margarine.

Bake in 325 degree oven until well set — about 45-50 minutes.

Egg with Brown Rice Casserole

1½ cups brown rice
3 teaspoons chopped chives
½ cup chopped pecans
1½ cups Royal yogurt
1 cup milk
½ cup chopped green pepper
1 cup yellow corn meal

1 cup Tillamook cheese
1 teaspoon sweet basil
½ stick salt-free margarine
6 hard-boiled eggs, shredded
Dulse or kelp

Cook rice 25 minutes. Mix in chives, pecans, Royal yogurt, milk, green pepper, corn meal, grated cheese, sweet basil (crushed between your palms). Cut margarine into small pieces and scatter in mixture. Fold in eggs. Flavor with dulse or kelp. Bake in oiled baking dish, 25-30 minutes at 350 degrees.

Makes 8-14 servings.

Baked Millet

1 cup millet
3 cups water
2 eggs
3 tablespoons raw sugar
1½ cups skim milk
¼ cup black manukka raisins

½ cup thinly sliced apples
3 tablespoons lemon juice
1 teaspoon nutmeg
½ stick unsalted margarine

Cook millet 35 minutes in the 3 cups of water. Cover and set aside. Beat the eggs and add sugar. Then add millet and milk alternately. Mix in all ingredients except margarine. Pour in eight-by-nine inch baking dish, lined with half of the margarine. Dot the other half on top. Bake in moderate oven, 325 degrees until set — 40-45 minutes.

Serve with plum or apricot jelly (see Potpourri).

Soy Casserole

½ cup chopped onions or chives
½ cup shredded carrots
½ cup chopped green peppers
1½ cups diced tomatoes
1 tablespoon Safflower oil
2 cups cooked soy beans
½ cup wheat germ
1 tablespoon Goodie high protein powder (or any protein powder)

1 teaspoon sweet paprika
1 teaspoon sweet basil
Dulse or kelp
¼ stick margarine
¼ cup raw sugar
¾ cup shredded Tillamook cheese

Saute onions, carrots, green peppers, tomatoes with oil for 15 minutes over low flame. Mix remaining ingredients except cheese.

Pour into well-oiled baking dish. Top with shredded cheese, cover, and bake at 325 degrees for 45 minutes.

Steamed Eggplant

1 pound eggplant, diced, unpeeled
½ cup chopped onions
2 tablespoons Safflower oil
1 cup diced green pepper
2 cups diced peeled tomatoes
1 clove garlic, chopped or pressed

1 cup Swiss chard
½ cup cold water
2 tablespoons whole wheat flour (level)
½ teaspoon sweet basil
1 tablespoon sugar
Kelp

Drop eggplant in boiling water for 2 minutes and strain. Saute the onions in the oil, add all the vegetables. Simmer about 15-20 minutes. Make thickening from the flour and water. Add to the vegetables, simmer 2 more minutes. Add sweet basil, sugar, and kelp to taste.

Egg and Rice Souffle

4 eggs
1 cup cooked brown rice
½ cup salt-free shredded Tillamook cheese
2 tablespoons light cream
1 teaspoon finely chopped fresh rosemary

Dulse or kelp powder to taste
½ cup finely chopped onions
2 tablespoons melted Safflower margarine

Beat eggs well in mixing bowl. Add remaining ingredients except onions and margarine. Saute the onions in the margarine. Combine all ingredients in a five-by-nine inch Pyrex loaf pan, greased with 2 tablespoons melted margarine.

Cover and bake in 300 degree oven until egg sets, about 20 minutes.

Protein Roast

1 cup dry lima beans
5 cups water
1 cup hulled millet
1 yam, ½ pound

½ cup chopped onions
2 tablespoons Safflower oil
½ cup cashew nuts
2 eggs, well beaten

Cook lima beans in three cups of water until tender. Cook millets in two cups of water and set aside. Boil yam in the jacket, cool and peel. Saute onions in the oil.

Add:

½ cup chopped
   mushrooms
¼ cup chopped green
   peppers

½ cup chopped Swiss
   chard

Simmer five minutes in ½ cup water.

Mash the cooked lima beans, millet, yam and cashew nuts in a mixing bowl, add onion mixture and well-beaten eggs. Add:

1 rounded tablespoon
   Torumel yeast powder
1 rounded tablespoon
   Goodie high protein
   powder (or any protein
   powder)

½ teaspoon marjoram
½ teaspoon tarragon
   leaves
Kelp or dulse

(Marjoram and tarragon leaves should be pulverized between your palms for better flavor.) Flavor with kelp or dulse.

Bake in eight-by-nine inch oiled baking dish, 325 degree oven until set (about 45 minutes).

Serve with Apple and Boysenberry Sauce (see Desserts).

Kale Leaf Stew

1 cup chopped onions	1 bunch kale leaves
2 tablespoons Safflower oil	½ teaspoon dulse

Saute the onions in the oil, wash and cut kale leaves small. Add to onions. Add:

1 cup diced turnips	1 clove garlic, chopped
1 cup diced cauliflower	or pressed
½ cup chopped green pepper	¼ teaspoon red paprika
	¼ teaspoon rosemary

Cook on low flame for twenty minutes. Add dulse. Serve with Tomato Sauce (see Sauces).

Okra and Corn

½ pound young okra	1 tablespoon Safflower oil
2 tablespoons tarragon vinegar	½ cup warm water
2 cups water	½ cup green pepper
2 cups corn kernels	1 cup peeled and diced tomatoes
¼ cup chopped onions	

Wash and cut the stems of the okra, cut in ½-inch pieces crosswise. Boil 2 cups of water in a sauce pan with tarragon vinegar. Drop in cut okra for 1 minute and drain.

Cut the fresh corn from the cob, in season, or use canned corn kernels. Saute the onions in the oil, add corn, ½ cup water and green pepper and cook until almost tender, add tomatoes and okra, cook it 5 more minutes. Make thickening from:

1 tablespoon whole wheat flour	¼ cup cold water

Add to the boiling okra, and simmer for 2 minutes. Flavor with:

½ tablespoon brown
sugar

Kelp

Stewed Tomatoes

1 cup chopped onions (not too fine)

2 tablespoons Safflower oil

6 medium tomatoes, peeled and diced

1 clove garlic, pressed

1 cup (2 slices) unsalted whole wheat bread, buttered with unsalted butter, toasted, and diced

Kelp or dulse

Saute the onions in the oil. Add all ingredients except the bread. Simmer ten to fifteen minutes until tomatoes and onions cook together. Add diced bread. Kelp or dulse added to taste is good with this dish.

Broiled Eggplant

1 eggplant (1 pound)

Wash and slice unpeeled eggplant ½ inch thick. Arrange slices in a nine-by-fourteen inch oiled baking dish. Brush with the following mixture:

4 tablespoons Safflower oil

1 tablespoon cider vinegar

½ teaspoon oregano

½ teaspoon dulse powder

1 clove garlic, pressed

Mix well all ingredients, brush top of the eggplant and broil to golden brown (about 6-8 minutes, according to how far from the flame). Turn and brush again and broil to golden brown.

Steamed Broccoli

1 bunch broccoli
½ stick unsalted
   margarine

1 tablespoon finely
   chopped onion
½ cup warm water

Wash and peel the stems of the broccoli. Cut off flowers and chop. Shred the stems. Melt the margarine in a heavy skillet. Add onions and saute. Add shredded stems and chopped flowers. Add water and mix. Cover and steam about ten minutes. Stir occasionally. You may need a little more water to avoid burning.

Serve hot.

Asparagus with Almond and Parsley Sauce

1½ pounds asparagus
3 cups water
⅓ cup melted Safflower
   margarine
1 tablespoon whole wheat
   flour

½ cup unsalted and
   blanched shredded
   almonds
1 tablespoon chopped
   parsley

Wash and break off the hard part of the asparagus, and cook in 3 cups of water until tender. Drain and save the liquid.

Mix melted margarine and flour in a sauce pan, heat well, stir to avoid burning. Pour on the drained cool liquid. Let it boil until thickened, stirring all the time. Take away from fire and add:

¼ cup lemon juice
1 teaspoon chopped
   chives

1 hard-boiled egg, diced
1 teaspoon brown sugar
½ teaspoon kelp powder

Mix well. Arrange asparagus on a square vegetable dish, pour over hot sauce. Sprinkle the top with shredded almonds and chopped parsley. Serve at once.

2 cups cut string beans	1 teaspoon kelp powder
½ cup chopped onions	2 tablespoons salt-free
1 cup cut celery	margarine
½ cup water	1 tablespoon chopped
½ cup sliced okra	fresh sweet basil

Steam string beans, onions, and celery in water, covered. After 10 minutes add okra. Cook 15 minutes. Before serving, add kelp, margarine, and basil.

Mushroom Sauce

½ cup chopped onions
2 tablespoons Safflower oil
1 cup chopped mushrooms
2½ cups vegetable broth
(see Soups)

3 tablespoons whole wheat
flour
½ cup cold water
Dulse

Saute the onions in the oil. Add mushrooms and let simmer 3 minutes. Heat the broth in a sauce pan. Make thickening from the whole wheat flour and ½ cup water. Add to the boiling broth, stirring constantly with a wire beater until you get the desired thickness.

Add mushrooms and onion mixture. Flavor with dulse. Serve on roasts and chop suey.

Tomato Sauce

¼ cup chopped onions
1 tablespoon Safflower oil
Dash of paprika
½ cup chopped green
pepper
3 cups tomato juice
⅔ cup water
3 tablespoons whole wheat
flour

¾ cup cold water
1 clove garlic, pressed
½ teaspoon sweet basil
¼ cup lemon juice
½ cup brown sugar
1 tablespoon honey
Dulse or kelp

Saute onions in the oil. Add dash of paprika and green peppers. Boil the tomato juice with the ⅔ cup of water. Make thickening from flour and cold water. Add slowly to boiling tomato juice. Simmer 2 minutes. Add onion mixture and remaining ingredients, stirring to avoid burning.

Serve on stuffed cabbage and roasts.

Parsley and Garlic Sauce

4 tablespoons Safflower oil   2 cups cold water
3 tablespoons whole
wheat pastry flour

In a 1 quart saucepan, heat the oil. Add the pastry flour, and stir over low flame until lightly browned.

¼ teaspoon red paprika   1 tablespoon finely
1 clove garlic, pressed or   chopped parsley
   finely chopped   Kelp to taste

Add the red pepper, garlic, and parsley. Then slowly add the 2 cups water, stirring constantly. Simmer 2 minutes, add kelp to taste.

Homemade Horseradish
(Easy to Make)

2 cups unpeeled finely   3 tablespoons brown
   shredded turnips   sugar
½ cup finely shredded   ½ cup cashew nuts,
   horseradish   ground
½ cup lemon juice

Wash turnips. Peel and wash horseradish. Shred on your salad maker, using the finest shredder.

Put in a small bowl, mix in lemon juice and sugar. Cover and let stand ½ hour. Combine with cashew nuts. Put in a jar and keep in refrigerator until used.

Sauce for Vegetables

¼ stick unsalted   ½ teaspoon sweet basil,
   margarine   pulverized between
4 tablespoons unbleached   palms
   flour   Kelp powder to taste
2 cups cold skim milk

Melt the margarine in a 1 quart saucepan. Add the un-bleached flour, blend and stir over low flame. Then gradually add the 2 cups of cold skim milk.

Cook until mixture lightly thickens. Stir constantly while cooking.

Then add the sweet basil. Flavor with kelp powder.

Hollandaise Sauce

¼ stick Safflower
   margarine
3 tablespoons whole wheat
   pastry flour

2 cups cold water

Melt the margarine in a 1 quart saucepan. Add flour, and cook on low flame, stirring constantly until light brown. Slowly pour in the water. Simmer 2 minutes. Add:

3 tablespoons lemon juice
1 tablespoon brown sugar

Dulse or kelp to taste

Remove from fire. Beat in:

2 egg yolks

Serve hot with asparagus or string beans.

Raisin Sauce

½ cup black manukka
   raisins

2½ cups water

Wash raisins. Cook in covered saucepan with the 2½ cups water for 10 minutes.

Make thickening from:

¾ cup cold water
4 tablespoons unbleached
  flour

Strain thickening and add to the boiling raisins. Simmer 2 minutes, stirring constantly. Remove from heat. Then add:

2 tablespoons lemon juice   1 egg yolk, beat in
2 tablespoons brown sugar

Serve with your favorite cake — it's delicious!

Whole Wheat Raisin Bread

2 tablespoons dry yeast   6 cups whole wheat flour
¾ cup warm water

Soak the yeast in the warm water. Sift the flour into a mixing bowl and set aside.

2 tablespoons honey   2 eggs, well beaten
2 tablespoons sugar   ½ cup black manukka
1 stick unsalted margarine   raisins
3 cups warm skim milk

Dissolve the honey, sugar, and margarine in the skim milk. Combine with the flour and add the eggs.

Wash and dry and add the raisins.

Make a fairly soft dough. Knead on a floured board until smooth and elastic. Cover and put back in a slightly oiled bowl and let rise until doubled in size. Form 3 loaves and bake in oiled Pyrex loaf pans. Bake at 325 degrees for 55 minutes.

Whole Grain Bread

6 cups whole wheat flour   5 cups warm water
3 cups rye flour   2 cakes yeast

Sift flour into a mixing bowl.

Soak the yeast in 1 cup warm water for 10 minutes until smooth. In the remaining 4 cups water, melt:

2 level tablespoons honey   ½ cup Safflower oil
2 level tablespoons brown   2 eggs, well beaten
  sugar

Using a wooden spoon, combine with the flour. Also add the yeast liquid to the mixture, and knead until smooth (about ½ hour). You may need a little more water to make a fairly soft dough. If you use electric mixer, leave the batter harder.

Sprinkle top with flour; cover with a towel; keep warm and let rise until doubled in bulk. Form 4 loaves and place in well-oiled loaf pans. Let rise again about ½ hour. Brush over with water and bake ¾ hour in a 350 degree oven.

Corn Bread

2¾ cups warm water	5½ cups unbleached flour
2 cups corn meal	3 teaspoons dry yeast

Pour 2 cups warm water on the corn meal. Dissolve yeast in the ¾ cup warm water. Sift unbleached flour into a mixing bowl. Add corn meal, then yeast. Add:

2½ cups skim milk	¾ cup Safflower oil
2 tablespoons honey	2 whole eggs, well beaten
1 tablespoon brown sugar	

Knead until dough is smooth and elastic. Sprinkle top with unbleached flour. Cover with a towel and let rise in a warm place until doubled in bulk. Fold on floured board. Put in oiled loaf pans; let rise ½ hour (in winter time, ¾ hour). Brush top with water and bake in 350 degree oven for 45 minutes.

Yield: three 1½ pound loaves.

Caraway Seed Bread

2 tablespoons caraway seeds	½ cup warm water
	4 cups unbleached flour
2 cups water	2 cups rye flour
1½ cakes yeast	1 egg, well beaten

In a saucepan, boil the caraway seeds in the 2 cups water for 10 minutes. Remove from heat, cover and set aside. Soak the yeast in the ½ cup warm water. Sift the flours into a mixing bowl.

Take the boiled caraway seeds and add enough water to make 3 cups liquid. Add:

½ cup Safflower oil   2 tablespoons honey
2 tablespoons brown sugar

With a wooden spoon, combine with the sifted flour and add the egg. Knead until smooth and elastic. Flour the top with unbleached flour. Cover with a towel and put in warm place. Let rise until doubled in size. Toss on floured board. Form 3 little loaves and let it rise again in oiled baking pans until it reaches the rim. Brush with cold water and bake in 325 degree oven for 55 minutes. Brush top again with cold water for even color.

Whole Wheat Bread
(Sponge Method)

1½ cakes yeast   3 cups water
¾ cup warm water
¾ pound Russett
   potatoes

Soak the yeast in ¾ cup water.

Wash the potatoes well. Boil in jackets in the 3 cups water. Save liquid. Peel and grate potatoes.

Sift the following into a mixing bowl:

5 cups whole wheat flour   2 cups unbleached flour

Using 2 cups of this mixture, in a separate bowl, make a well in the middle; and with a tablespoon paddle the soaked yeast into the flour. Make a sponge. Sprinkle the top with flour, cover and let rise until doubled in size.

In a saucepan, take the water from the boiled potatoes and add enough water to make 3 cups liquid. To this add grated potatoes and:

2 tablespoons sugar   ½ cup Safflower oil
2 tablespoons honey

Mix well and combine with the sponge and flour. Make a fairly stiff dough. By using the potato water, the dough is looser and easier to knead. Fold the edges to the middle and press with your fist. Flour it lightly to prevent it from sticking. Knead until little bubbles come up and give a sound like a whistle. Then you know the dough is well kneaded. Flour the top lightly, cover with a towel and let rise in a warm place until doubled in size. Place on a lightly floured board. Make four loaves and place in oiled loaf pans. Let it rise until it reaches the rim of the pan. Brush with cold water and bake in 325 degree oven for 55 minutes.

Honey Cookies

1 stick Safflower margarine
½ cup brown sugar
2 eggs, beaten
2 cups whole wheat
   pastry flour

2 teaspoons baking
   powder
½ cup honey
1 cup chopped walnuts
½ teaspoon vanilla

Cream margarine. Add sugar and mix into margarine. Add eggs one by one and beat. Add flour (sifted with the baking powder) and remaining ingredients.

Form into roll, wrap in wax paper, and chill in refrigerator until firm.

Cut thin slices about ½ inch thick and bake on floured cookie sheet for ten to twelve minutes at 375 degrees.

Yield: 30 cookies.

Carob Marble Cake

2¼ cups whole wheat
   pastry flour
2½ teaspoons baking
   powder
6 egg yolks
1½ cups brown sugar

½ cup cold water
½ cup Safflower oil
2 teaspoons vanilla
6 egg whites
½ teaspoon cream of
   tartar

Sift flour in a mixing bowl with the baking powder. Add egg yolks, sugar, water, Safflower oil, and vanilla. Mix well with a wooden spoon until smooth.

Beat the egg whites with the cream of tartar and fold gently into the batter.

Pour the mixture in a well-oiled and floured tube pan. Grease the pan, using Safflower oil.

To make the marble use:

¾ cup brown sugar
6 tablespoons plain carob powder

1 teaspoon vanilla
½ cup boiling water

Mix the sugar, carob powder , and vanilla into the hot water and spoon all around the batter. Swirl around with a narrow knife through the batter to form marbled pattern.

Bake thirty minutes in preheated 325 degree oven, then raise oven temperature to 350 for twenty more minutes.

Oatmeal Cookies

1 stick Safflower margarine
1½ cups brown sugar

1 egg

Cream margarine and sugar. Add egg and beat well. Add:

1½ cups unbleached flour (sifted)
2 teaspoons baking powder

1 teaspoon cinnamon
½ teaspoon powdered cloves

Sift once more. Add to the egg mixture. Then add:

1½ cups rolled oats
½ cup skim milk

½ cup black manukka raisins

Drop by teaspoonfuls on oiled cookie sheet. Bake in 350 degree oven for 20 minutes.

Yield: about 30 cookies.

Honey Cake

1 cup honey	6 egg whites
1 cup brown sugar	
6 egg yolks	
1¾ cups unbleached or whole wheat pastry flour	

Beat honey and brown sugar smooth. Add egg yolks one by one and beat well. Sift the flour, then measure 1¾ cups. Add to honey mixture along with:

⅓ cup orange juice	1 teaspoon vanilla
½ teaspoon powdered cloves	

Beat 6 egg whites stiff and fold gently into the mixture. Bake in oiled and floured tube pan in 325 degree oven for fifty minutes.
Serve with peppermint tea.

Refrigerator Walnut Cookies

2 eggs	1 teaspoon vanilla extract
1¼ cups brown sugar	
¾ cup soft unsalted margarine	

Mix ingredients above until creamy.

1½ cups whole wheat pastry flour	1½ teaspoons baking powder

Sift together and add to the egg and sugar mixture. Refrigerate 1 hour for easy handling. Then shape dough into 24 or more little balls. Combine:

¾ cup ground walnuts   ½ teaspoon cinnamon
½ cup brown sugar

Roll each ball in the mixture. Place 2 inches apart on an oiled cookie sheet. Bake in 300 degree oven for 20 minutes, until golden brown.

Carob Chocolate Crunch

1 stick Safflower   1½ cups brown sugar
  margarine   2 eggs, well beaten

Cream margarine, mix well with sugar and eggs.

2 cups whole wheat pastry   ½ cup warm water
  flour   1 teaspoon vanilla
½ teaspoon baking soda   ½ teaspoon cinnamon

Add the flour; dissolve baking soda in water, and add, along with the vanilla and cinnamon. Mix well. Add:

1 cup small diced carob   ½ cup chopped walnuts
  powder candy

Mix well. Make little balls, and press to make flat, round cookies. Top each with 1 walnut quarter.

Baked Rice Pudding

½ stick Safflower margarine	2 eggs (separated)
6 tablespoons brown sugar	

Cream margarine with the sugar. Add egg yolks one by one and beat well until smooth and creamy.

Add:

2 cups milk	⅓ teaspoon nutmeg
2 cups boiled brown rice	2 tablespoons lemon juice
2 tablespoons dry currants	1 teaspoon lemon rind

Mix well. Beat the two egg whites stiff, and fold in gently.

Pour mixture in a well-oiled eight-by-nine inch baking dish. Dot with Safflower margarine. Bake in moderate 300 degree oven until top is golden brown.

Rice and Prune Pudding (or Zimmes)

1 cup brown rice	½ teaspoon cinnamon
3 cups water	1 cup cooked and pitted prunes
2 eggs	
1 cup brown sugar	½ stick Safflower margarine
1½ cups skim milk	

Wash rice and cook it in 3 cups water until tender. Cover and set aside.

Beat the eggs well with a wire beater. Add sugar, mix well, add rice, milk, and cinnamon.

Pour mixture into eight-by-nine inch oiled baking dish and dot with the prunes and margarine.

Bake in 350 degree oven for 35-40 minutes until set.

Banana Bread

5 egg yolks
1 cup brown sugar
2 tablespoons Safflower oil
2 cups whole wheat flour

1½ teaspoons baking powder
¾ cup buttermilk

Beat egg yolks, sugar and oil to a smooth texture. Sift flour and baking powder and add to egg mixture. Also add buttermilk. Add:

2 ripe bananas, mashed (1 cup)
½ cup walnuts, coarsely chopped

2 teaspoons vanilla
¼ teaspoon powdered cloves
5 egg whites

Mix lightly. Beat the egg whites stiff, and fold in gently.
Bake in oiled and floured twelve-by-eight inch baking dish in 350 degree oven for twenty minutes; then lower oven temperature to 325 degrees and continue baking thirty minutes longer.
Let cool before slicing.

Apple Cobbler

6 medium tart apples
1 cup water
1 cup brown sugar, packed
½ teaspoon cinnamon
½ cup black manukka raisins

3 tablespoons lemon juice
¼ stick Safflower margarine

Wash and core apples. Cut in half and slice each half in 6 pieces. Arrange cut apples in an eight-by-nine inch baking dish. Pour on 1 cup of water. Mix remaining ingredients, except margarine, and sprinkle on the apples. Dot with margarine.

Cover with the following pie dough:

1 stick Safflower margarine	¼ teaspoon baking powder
1¼ cups whole wheat pastry flour	1 egg, well beaten
	¼ cup cold water

Rub margarine with the flour and baking powder (sifted together). Add beaten egg and water. Mix lightly. Fold on floured board and roll out to the size of the baking dish. Roll up on the rolling pin and roll out on top of the baking dish, starting at the edge. Brush top with egg yolk.

Punch a few times with a fork — to avoid bubbling up. Bake in 350 degree oven until golden brown (about 45 minutes).

Apples and Apricot Delight

6 medium-sized juicy apples, pared and sliced thin	½ cup dried apricots, soaked in 1 cup of water

Arrange a row of sliced apples in an oiled eight-by-nine inch Pyrex dish; then a row of soaked apricots, cut into 4 pieces.

Mix:

2 tablespoons honey	¼ cup lemon juice

Sprinkle over fruit. Then add the following topping:

1 cup cashew nuts, ground, or whole pine nuts	½ teaspoon cinnamon
1 cup rolled oats	½ stick Safflower margarine
4 rounded tablespoons brown sugar	

149

Sweeten the oats with the brown sugar, flavored with the cinnamon. Melt the margarine; mix with oats and top the fruit.

Bake in 300 degree moderate oven for thirty-five to forty minutes until the topping is a golden brown.

Boysenberry and Apple Sauce

1 package frozen boysenberries

6 tablespoons lemon juice

½ cup 100% maple syrup

6 medium apples, cored, cut into small pieces

Thaw the berries and put in the blender for three minutes until smooth. Strain and return to blender. Add lemon juice, syrup and apples slowly. Blend until smooth.

Boysenberry or Other Berry Juices
(Very Refreshing on Hot Summer Days)

If you don't have fresh, use frozen berries.

3 rounded tablespoons raw
  sugar
16 ounces water

1 pound boysenberries
10 drops berry extract

Dissolve sugar in water. Place berries in blender with a little water. Make a smooth liquid. Then strain out the seeds. Place the liquid in blender, add sugar and extract and run for 3-4 minutes.

Then strain and cool in refrigerator. When cooled, add 8 ounces of apple juice, if desired.

Tortillas with Avocado

1 cup hot water
½ cup corn meal

2 eggs

Pour hot water on corn meal. Cover and set aside. Beat the eggs in blender for 2 seconds (should not be foamy). Add:

1½ cups skim milk
1 cup whole wheat flour
1 cup unbleached flour

2 tablespoons Safflower
  oil

Blend, stir well; then add corn meal and water and blend smooth.

Heat a six-inch skillet, oiled with a paper towel to take off the excess oil. Pour in enough to cover the bottom of the skillet, tip both ways for even thickness. Bake on both sides to golden brown.

Yield: 12 little tortillas.

Filling

2 cups diced avocado
1 cup diced tomatoes
1 cup diced cucumber
1 cup diced Cheddar
   cheese
1 tablespoon chopped
   scallions
½ cup green pepper

1 cup chopped romaine
   lettuce
1 teaspoon dulse
2 tablespoons Lecinaise or
   mayonnaise
¼ cup lime or lemon
   juice

Mix all ingredients in a mixing bowl except mayonnaise and lemon or lime juice. Dissolve the mayonnaise in the lemon or lime juice and add. Fill tortillas.

Refreshing High Protein Drink

10 ounces water
2 rounded tablespoons skim
   milk powder
1 rounded tablespoon
   Goodie high protein
   powder (other protein
   powder may be substituted)

2 rounded tablespoons
   unsalted cashew nuts
Dash of cinnamon
Honey for sweetening — 1
   teaspoon (or according
   to your taste)
1 rounded tablespoon
   sunflower seeds

Mix water, skim milk, and protein powder in blender until smooth. Add the nuts, sunflower seeds, and cinnamon. Run blender a few minutes at low speed. Then add honey and run blender at high speed until smooth.

Apricot Jelly

¾ cup dry unsulphured   1 cup hot water
  apricots

Soak apricots in hot water until all water is absorbed.
Put in blender and add:

2 tablespoons lemon juice   2 tablespoons brown sugar
3 tablespoons orange   ½ teaspoon apricot
  blossom honey   extract

Blend to smooth texture.
Cool in refrigerator before serving.

Fruit Soup, Number 1

½ cup dry apricots   6 cups water
½ cup dry peaches   1 cup pineapple juice
½ cup dry pears   unsweetened
1 piece whole cinnamon

Cook the fruit in six cups of water until tender. Cut
in small pieces, add pineapple juice. Beat in blender:

1 cup yogurt   2 tablespoons honey
2 tablespoons lemon juice   2 tablespoons brown sugar

Add to the fruit.
Serve cold with extra yogurt on top.

¼ cup lemon juice
1 cup diced fresh
  peaches
½ cup pitted cherries, cut
  in half
1 cup diced apples
½ cup diced pears

3 tablespoon 100%
  maple syrup
1½ cups water
6 tablespoons yogurt
1 pint apple juice
1 pint grape juice

Parboil the lemon juice, peaches, cherries, apples, pears and maple syrup in the 1½ cups water.

Mix apple and grape juice. Put 1½ cups of the juice mixture in blender, blend with the yogurt. Blend in the fruit and the remaining fruit juice.

Serve cold with extra yogurt on top.

INDEX

BOOK ONE

DELICIOUS COOKBOOKS
FROM PAPERBACK LIBRARY!